Supercow Publishing

Lewes, De 2021

Leading Educators Made Simple

Steven Lucas

*Principles and practices you can put to work today to be a
more effective educational leader.*

CHAPTER 1

Leading Made Simple

We can build a great argument the times we are living through right now in America and perhaps the World are amongst the most turbulent and perplexing in recent history. Even before being hit over the head with a global pandemic, the world was wrestling with challenges presented by issues of social justice and environmental, cultural, and economic angst. Ironically, these issues and many others have been exacerbated by technology, which while having the potential to solve many problems, instead seems to create new conditions of access, confusion, and proximity never before imagined.

Unlike previous times in our history (think 911 and the way the event galvanized us- even temporarily), recent events have driven us further apart than they have together. Our society has devolved into a polarized, even binary entity with two schools of thought and little in between. The overarching theme is, "you are either for us or against us, and if you do not believe in what we believe, you are wrong". This, unfortunately, seems to be the sentiment of many people and organizations. Our world has picked sides making everything more difficult. These conditions have created an ever increasing need for people to be able to form and lead teams to collaborate and solve problems. These problems include those of today, but also those which have not even been thought of yet.

Fortunately, people by themselves are the most amazing and intelligent beings we know of in the universe. Even better, people joined together on a team, for a common purpose, with great leadership will increase the capabilities of the people by themselves exponentially. High quality, well-led teams can and have literally performed miracles, and this is not an overstatement. History is riddled with evidence of human intellect and invention intensified when joined for a

common purpose and provided with great leadership. Now,

as much as any time before, we need great leaders to step up

and get us through these turbulent and perplexing days.

The good news is, leaders are everywhere. Look

around! While most of the people we see we do not always

qualify as leaders, there are leaders all around. Some leaders

in our communities are easy to see like the school board

member, Police Chief, Politician, or Coach. Other leaders are

not as easy to pick out but have just as much authority and

influence as those we more traditionally identify as leaders.

These are the hidden leaders among us who are called on to

lead every day but do not even know it.

When I think of these hidden leaders, I think of

people like parents who lead their families through a variety

of challenges. Whether it is one parent at home, organizing

things, shopping, driving the kids here or there, the other

parent driving off to work each day to make a living, or one parent alone trying to do the work of both, parents are serving their families as leaders of their team. Parents are the first leaders our children see and probably their biggest influencers. Parenting requires leadership skills.

I also think about the teachers who take charge of their classrooms and lead students throughout the day. While many teachers will feign from being called "leader", think of the pure leadership it takes to command and direct numbers of school children each day for nearly 200 days a year! And, what about the business owners both large and small who make countless decisions each day about everything from soup to nuts, or our pastors or other faith directors who lead us to believe? They are all leaders in our culture and rely on certain skills and tendencies to get them through their tasks of leading and influencing other groups of people to achieve certain ends.

What is Leadership?

While countless studies have been conducted, and a myriad of theories about leadership have been proposed, the effect of leadership on an organization is still difficult to quantify. Yet, all of us who have been on any kind of team or belonged to any organization know the leader of every team makes a decided impact on the morale, effectiveness, and overall outcomes of the group they lead. The question we all seek to have definitively answered is why are some people able to lead and inspire others to reach their highest potential of growth and output, while others seem to just coast along or even digress or disintegrate great teams? Since you are probably in a leadership position, you want to know how to better influence your team to succeed. You want to know what the skills are to better do your job and serve your communities.

This is very likely why an infinite number of pages have been written, podcasts have been broadcasted, trainings have been created and conducted, companies formed, and experts have been (mostly) self-identified about the topic of leadership. The fact is, leadership, while easy to judge as either amazing or horrible, is very difficult to accurately analyze even from a research perspective. Most experts will say leadership is such a complex and situational subject, it is just too hard to define the practices which work. The conditions, mission, and personnel being led create too many variables.

Moreover, while we all see and know someone we think is a great leader, sometimes knowing exactly why the person can get others to respond without question is a mystery. It just seems like while the many great leaders we see all have the ability to get things done, they do it in very different ways. Some do it with force, others with finesse.

Some command instant respect, while others take time to get to know. Some are great orators or tell inspirational stories, while others scripted and even dry. Some we follow because we want to, others unfortunately, because we have to.

What you can expect to find here

If you have picked up this book, you are undoubtedly interested in knowing how to tap into your own existing skills and expand your abilities to become a better educational leader. This is commendable and demonstrates a commitment to improve your impact on both the people you serve, and the outcomes of your team or organization. Hopefully, what you find here will both simplify this very complex and even mysterious topic while feeding your desire to improve.

Just a word of warning. What you will not find in this book is a research project or dissertation summarized in a *how-to* format. Although, I have included several stories I

have read or learned about including the actions or behaviors

of some historical figures, this is not a literary analysis of

anyone's biography. Nor is it a scientific assessment of

leadership attributes which if applied will give you x, y, or z

value of succeeding. What you will find in this book is an

experienced-based review of leadership traits and practices

which I have observed to work while spending nearly 40

years of working as and observing leaders. Of course, much

of the guidance in this book is also based on training and

doctrine, much of which I derived during my time serving as a

Marine. I use the term *Leading Made Simple* throughout the

book to qualify ideas which are singularly a product of this

work. In other words, while based on other theory and

practice, *Leading Made Simple* practices are my own

recommendations.

I wholeheartedly disagree with the notion there are no *born leaders,* but contend there are only limited exceptions to this premise. Abraham Lincoln comes to mind who, among many other great early leadership accomplishments, had to look after his young sister for seven months at the age of nine while his father went off to Kentucky to find a new wife. Later as a boy, he was known to go down to the local court house, review court cases and then cite them from memory as he told the most interesting of the cases to his young friends. While Lincoln showed early evidence of natural leadership, people like him are pretty rare.

The good news is, most researchers agree leadership is a skill which can be learned, improved, and implemented into practice by everyone willing to work at it. Also, it is far more likely, the great majority of leaders develop based on their training and experiences. This is wonderful for the majority of us who are not those few born leaders who just seem to have innate and uncommonly high skills of integrity, intelligence, confidence, and charisma to naturally influence large swaths of people.

How to use this

This book is designed to combine theory and practice with some hopefully enjoyable stories and anecdotes. Many of these stories are based on my personal experiences as a Marine, a teacher, and a leader, and others are based on interesting things I have read or heard. They are mostly true but like all Marine stories some of them might have a bit of spice added just to increase the lore. I promise there is no harm and the general meaning is unchanged. At the end of each chapter, I sum things up and offer a couple of easy ideas to activate the things you have read. I have tried to make these activities useful so you can take advantage of them individually or as a team if you are reading this with a group of other leaders. You can also just think about them if you prefer, and move on to the next chapter.

The Author

If you are the type of skeptic who needs to be convinced the author of this book is worthy of giving you advice about leadership, there is a short bio at the end of the book. Hopefully, you'll get a feel for my capacity as a leader long before then. While many authors will try to convince you to keep reading by listing their achievements and accomplishments in the front of their book, I have saved my short and very modest list of accomplishments for the back. While it makes perfect sense that anyone interested in learning how to be a better leader does not want to waste time learning from someone who lacks credibility, it similarly makes sense you do not want your time wasted reading the common boasting and personal hyperbole with which the many writers will fill the first few chapters of their book.

Therefore, I have left my credentials and experiences on which I based this book for last, leaving it to the reader to decide when they want to review those qualifications. It is my hope you choose to read this book based on the topic and not the author.

The basis on which I have written this book while pragmatic, still maintains a philosophical view on leadership. I say this work is pragmatic because I know as a leader, we all want to read something we can put into practice immediately. While we all would probably love to read more for entertainment, most of us who read about a topic like leadership want to be informed and given suggestions we can implement today. I say the book is philosophical because I maintain that while I will give you many practical things you can do immediately to improve your leadership practices, many of these practices will be hard to measure at first and take time to see. I assure you though, all of which is written here works even if it is not backed up by a dissertation or research project.

For example, if you are in an organization which has suffered under poor or even mediocre leadership, the people on the team are often like someone who is wounded or suffering from an illness. Worse, they are often so habituated to working under the conditions, they do not know any better and they will resist the tenets of goods leadership even when it clearly makes their lives better. In other words, they will resist the medicine which will heal their wound or cure their illness. This takes time, faith, and persistence to change.

Let me give you a personal example from an experience told to me by a friend of mine. After my career in the Marine Corps I was excited to begin a second career as a teacher. I worked hard to complete an undergraduate degree before retiring from active duty and landed my first job teaching in a fantastic school district. Since my military

training made me accustomed to working my way up into

leadership, I earned a Master of Education Degree, and after

doing some post-graduate work, I found myself a school

administrator (leader) within a few years. I later worked my

way up to becoming a high school principal, and eventually

earned a Doctorate of Education and became a District

Superintendent.

Before choosing to pursue a career in school

leadership though, I was cautioned by a friend of mine who

had made the leap several years earlier. My friend recounted

for me how his first experience as a school leader had gone.

In his first school leadership assignment, he followed in his

new role, an exceptional educator and school leader. For the

purpose of this book only, we will refer to this leader as Dr.

Ted. Dr. Ted was so well qualified and accomplished, he led

for many years and was highly respected by many whom he

led and most, if not all, the people he did not lead. He is still, to this day, one of the people, many educational leaders try to emulate as they lead their schools and districts. Imagine my friend's challenge of following a leader who was so well-respected and well-established as a school and community leader? He was going to have to be very effective immediately or risk losing the respect of the community, the staff, and his peers quickly.

Compounding the difficulty of following a leader of such excellence was that Dr. Ted and my friend were polar opposites in their styles of leadership. Dr. Ted was extremely detailed and task oriented. He knew every person's job better than they did themselves. He knew the answer to every question he asked before any subordinate could answer and left very little up for discussion. This guy had been at it a long time, was better at it than most, and made sure everyone knew it.

Dr. Ted ran ceremonies like a West Point Parade. He was the Emcee and left little to nothing to chance. He gave every signal, introduced every speaker, and personally supervised every detail. Anything which disrupted or interfered with the pomp and ceremony, decorum, or precision of the event was addressed harshly during the post-event conference. Those who did not live up to his standards were addressed and often permanently marked as incompetent.

The staff was accustomed to making no decisions and being told everything they needed to know and do. As a result, the school operated very effectively. Compliance was high which, my friend recounted, was one of the measures the staff saw as very important. Thus, was the life at this school which was mostly high performing and very highly compliant. Despite this, there was an underlying but obvious "something" missing.

Unfortunately, while compliance at my friend's new

school was high, productivity, morale, and most importantly

the relationships between the staff, community, and

students were only marginal. There were numerous

conflicting camps within the school. Many worshipped Dr.

Ted and appreciated his "tight ship" and the way he told

them to think, act, and comply. In fact, they expected this.

Many knew no different and saw this as exceptional

leadership. The departments which adhered to Dr. Ted's

methods were the most highly respected and shone brightly

above the others and he recognized them enthusiastically for

their allegiance.

Students were treated the same way. There were

three distinct groups of students. Those who were the best

followers, earned the awards and accolades. They were in all

of the yearbook pictures and led the clubs, teams, and

sports. The second group of students were less likely to buy-in and typically just coasted along unencumbered. The third group of students (of which there was a large number), pushed back against this strong traditional way of playing school. Often, they became discipline problems and many underachieved.

Initiative and innovation in this school were scorned, certain students and staff ostracized, and the culture was rotten. This was particularly challenging for the new leader as his approach to leadership was the opposite of the overbearing, micromanaging style of Dr. Ted. Ironically, my friend had the reputation as a no-nonsense disciplinarian yet he was the one who avoided a one way, top-down leadership style.

While Dr. Ted's style of knowing and doing everything is more common amongst many school leaders than not (for too many reasons to cover here), every leadership book ever written discourages this kind of leadership. In fact, if you sat in on one of Dr. Ted's excellent sessions on leadership, he himself would discourage his own practices, instead professing collaboration, inclusive thought, and decentralized leadership as the preferred method of leading schools and districts! Nevertheless, this was the situation when my good friend and colleague walked into his first school leadership challenge. Needless to say, he had to change some deeply held convictions and allegiances to affect the culture and improve the morale. His first order of business was to encourage a "we" instead of "me" mentality.

It was not easy. My friend's philosophy of letting professionally trained, well-equipped personnel do their jobs to the best of their abilities with the least possible restrictions is foreign to many leaders in the education community. The new leader's unwillingness to make everyone's decisions for them and tell them every simple thing they needed to know about how to do their jobs took some getting used to for this staff. My friend was shocked at being bombarded regularly with questions of "can I do this or can I do that?", while subordinate leaders were left completely out of the conversation. The chain of command was literally a totem pole with the Dr. Ted at the top and everyone and everything needing his approval.

The staff insisted on being told everything. They were used to a weekly update in which even staff absences were posted. While most teaching staffs will complain about the frequency of staff meetings, this one pushed back when my friend chose to limit them. Their anxiety was evident if they did not get regular updates about things for which they had no control nor were they even effected by. Their standard tool for student discipline was to write a student referral to the office for every nominal offense and then expect administrators to not only "fix" the student, but then provide a full explanation of the consequences assigned by the administration. The staff was married to procedure and little else mattered. This created a culture where most complied, and those who did not were labeled as poor performers or worse.

This book is not about some dramatic turn around or feel-good story about how a new leader came galloping in on a faithful steed and made everything alright. The truth is, the school in the above story was high-performing where many educators would want to spend their careers. Yet, there were a lot of ways good leadership could make the school culture better and the new leadership team did. In virtually every statistical category, the school my friend led in this case improved. Most importantly, the school became a community. People liked being there and felt empowered to make the school a better place to work and learn. To do this, the leader did not have to make some dramatic programmatic changes, fire a bunch of people, or give a bunch of motivating speeches. The leader relied on his understanding of foundational leadership practices in this leadership role and made a difference. Those practices are herein and I encourage you to read on and start putting them into practice today.

Before moving on, I want to clarify a bit of the text of this work. I use the word "boss" on occasion to describe the leader of a group or organization. I understand some folks object to the word for one reason or another. If this word offends you, or you are someone who feels like the word is outdated or understates the value of a leader's role or the relationship he or she has with the team, I apologize. Please try to overlook it. Next, I have tried to make this work gender neutral. If it is interpreted in any way otherwise, I also apologize. I have served with and for many great men and great women leaders. Both men and women can lead effectively and history is rich with examples of both.

Summing things up

Our world may have never had a greater need for people to form and lead teams. While there are probably some "born leaders" most people develop their ability to lead others through experience and training. The proof is that there are leaders everywhere we look. Moms and dads, teachers, police officers, and small business owners are just a few. Much research has been conducted on leadership and what leaders do. Despite this, good leadership is still somewhat of a mystery although most can see and judge whether leadership is bad or good. This book provides both a pragmatic and philosophical perspective on leadership. Those interested in immediate takeaways and those who just find leadership an interesting topic can both find something here. Whatever your motive, you should be commended for reading and using your skills as a leader to help lead teams of people to make this complex and often perplexing world a

better place.

Putting this in to Practice

Reflection Question: What is your purpose in reading about

becoming a better leader and what do you expect to draw

from the information here?

Suggestions for Action: Think about some of the specific

challenges you have as a leader right now. Make a list of the

skills you think you need to best navigate those challenges.

Then, think about some of the best and worst leaders you

have seen in your life. Reflect on the factors in which these

leaders

differ. Finally, reflect on the qualities they had which were

similar.

CHAPTER 2

Leadership Indicators

The United States Marine Corps exemplifies leadership. In fact, one of the first things our Marines learn is when more than one Marine is in one place, someone is in charge. Marines rely on the concept of leadership to succeed and the Corps explicitly teaches Marines the most important thing they will ever do is lead their fellow Marines on the battlefield. Because of this, Marines love and embrace the concept of leadership. They study it, practice it, and have weeks and months long schools which teach leadership at every level. To Marines, leadership is a science and they hone their abilities to lead constantly. To start a discussion about leadership, the Marines are a good example of what exactly leadership is and how we know when it is effective.

In many ways, we can see good leadership, but to measure it is much more difficult. The term *leadership indicator* is used throughout this text to identify the things which suggest effective, or successful leadership. These are the measuring sticks. We can also look at these indicators as the absolute minimum objects leaders must accomplish. When leaders do these things, they have technically met the standards of effective leadership. In other words, this is precisely what leaders do to succeed.

The Marine Corps recognizes two indicators of successful leadership: Mission accomplishment and troop welfare. Marines will tell you that mission accomplishment is by far the most important of the two. Leaders in the Marines never like to lose a fellow Marine to the enemy, but unfortunately, sometimes the cost of accomplishing their mission results in the loss of life, hence mission accomplishment overshadowing troop welfare as their premier leadership indicator. This is why Marines will immediately evaluate what amounts to accomplishing their mission before they start any task. Knowing the desired outcome guides their development of even the simplest of plans.

Still, Marines know the mission cannot be accomplished without the men and women on the ground. Thus, the second indicator of leadership is troop welfare. Never have I been associated with an organization which takes the welfare of their people more seriously than the Marine Corps. Marine leaders are charged with knowing their people and employing them within their abilities. They keep up with their subordinates' medical and dental readiness, take ownership over their training, and advise them on career goals. This is just not how some Marine leaders operate, this type of caring leadership is a staple and mandate for every person in any position of leadership. Marines know the readiness of their troops and the effectiveness of their force depends on them getting paid, trained, fed, and cared for. Thus, the importance of troop welfare and its impact on leadership effectiveness.

Mission Accomplishment

Marines are so committed to mission accomplishment, it is the foundation of virtually everything they do. Every element of every operation, training, and evaluation has an emphasis on mission accomplishment. No matter the task, Marines want to know and understand their mission and how they can demonstrate it has been accomplished. In fact, Marines will commonly report back to their superior with the response of "mission accomplished" when finishing up a task or assignment.

Here is an example which illustrates how serious Marines take their understanding of their mission. The mission of the Marine Rifle Squad is to "*locate, close with, and destroy the enemy by fire and maneuver, and repel the enemy's assaults by fire and close combat*" (MCIP 3-10A.4i w/Change 1). Pretty simple. Marines know they have two jobs. First, find and destroy the enemy. Second, defend against them when necessary.

The point of writing this is, even though I have provided a reference, I personally did not need one. I assume most other former Marines would not need a reference to quote the mission of the Marine Rifle Squad either. I learned the mission of the Marine rifle squad nearly forty years ago as a Marine recruit and remember it verbatim to this day. The Marine Corps made sure I knew it and made regular references to it throughout my career. Conversely, since my retirement in 2003, I have worked in numerous professional organizations and do not remember any of their mission statements. In most other organizations of which I have been a member, I am not sure they even had a mission statement. The idea of not only having a mission statement, but knowing it, and actually accomplishing the mission is uncommonly high in the Marine Corps and unfortunately foreign to many other organizations.

Marines are also what we call, "mission oriented". They give and understand "mission orders" (also called "mission type orders"), and expect everyone in the chain of command to make decisions which support and ensure the mission is accomplished. Marines may also be the originators of "backwards planning" as they start every discussion or planning meeting with their mission and work back from there. They do not leave anything to chance as to what the mission is and what qualifies as mission accomplishment. A clear standard for mission accomplishment is their starting point.

Here is one example of a Marine accomplishing his mission. Louis B. "Chesty" Puller is perhaps the most decorated and famous Marine. "Chesty" Puller rose to the rank of Lieutenant General and likely would have been

Commandant of the Marine Corps had it not been for his open mind and willingness to share it. A recipient of five Navy Crosses, the second highest award for valor in the armed forces, to say Chesty Puller is a legend and icon to Marines would be shortchanging his legend greatly. There are countless references to "Chesty" throughout Marine culture including even naming their iconic mascot, an English bulldog, after him. Chesty Puller *is* the Marine Corps.

In 1950, the 1st Marine Division was engaged at the Chosin Reservoir in Korea. Aptly, nicknamed the "frozen Chosin" due to the harsh cold, snow, ice, and general misery, the Marines found themselves surrounded by a sizeable force of Chinese regular army. Puller, then a Colonel, was leading the 1st Marine regiment and was greatly outnumbered, outgunned, and undersupplied. The only option for Puller was to pull back, but finding he was completely surrounded, even retreat was not a viable option.

Besides, Chesty Puller was not one to ever consider retreating despite the odds.

To answer his Regiment's dilemma, Puller engineered what was later termed a "fighting withdrawal". Gathering all his Marines and equipment, Puller faced his men about, pointing their weapons through the rear of his entrenched Marines and fought their way back to safety of the larger American forces. When told he was completely surrounded, Puller is said to have responded, "Great. Now we can just shoot in every direction."

Puller's actions are indicative of the latitude given Marine leaders to make decisions based on the tactical conditions in order to accomplish a greater mission. Puller knew challenging the enemy who so vastly outnumbered him was going to result in many casualties, but he also knew staying in place and sacrificing his force to both the freezing conditions and overwhelming forces, would cause even greater harm to his unit. Losing or being captured would

have even been more detrimental to the overall success of

the entire Allied Forces in Korea and the outcome of the war-

not to mention the reputation of the Marine Corps itself and

its storied history. Puller seized the initiative given to him by

his understanding of the mission and his authority to lead,

and many of his Marines survived.

Simon Sinek calls this determining your "why". In his

book *Start with Why*, Sinek defines the why as "the purpose,

cause or belief that drives every one of us" (Sinek, 2011). He

further teaches us that the "what" the "how" and the "why"

are all linked to our brain and the chemical decision making

process (Sinek, 2011). For the Marines the mission is the

"why". It makes perfect sense that people are way more apt

to do something when they know "why" they are doing it. In

the case of the Marines, the collective "why" is exponentially

more powerful than any individual "why". In other words

when everyone is made very clear on the "why" and they all
have the same motive, everything everyone does in support
of accomplishing it.

I have seen in many poorly led organizations that the
selfish, personal beliefs of the individuals in the workforce
will outweigh the collective outcomes of the organization
causing division and impacting productivity and success.
Worse is when teams of people join in cliques and groups of
conflicting goals which actually work against each other.
Imagine now if everyone in your school or organization was
collectively behind accomplishing the same mission instead
of just determining what was important for them and only
doing that? This is why clarifying the mission is so important
and insisting that accomplishing the organization's mission is
not optional. This is also why organizational mission
statements need to be crafted with input from all of the
stakeholders and then be interwoven throughout all

elements of planning and training. For the mission to get

accomplished, everyone needs to buy in and be committed

to completing it.

One of the first things a leader should do for every

situation is to identify exactly what the mission

(outcome/why/product) is for the particular event, problem,

or team. If I am assigned to lead a committee for example,

my first question is always, "OK, what exactly is our mission?"

Or, "What exactly are we going to accomplish?" If the rest of

the committee does not know, cannot define it, or if we are a

new committee, we need to define the end state for

ourselves before we can embark on a plan to make it

happen. Clarifying the mission works for short term things

like planning a *back to school* night or professional

development session, medium range things like improving

quarterly discipline or grades, or longer range things like

improving graduation rates. Leaders should always start with the mission and work backwards from there.

As an example, I had the pleasure of working in an outstanding school district as a school leader. Our school, while very good, lagged behind many of the other schools in our district in several areas. One area I was particularly concerned about was the rate at which our students graduated from high school. Even though the students in our school were every bit as capable and competent as those in our neighboring schools, our graduation rate was several percentage points behind. To me this was unacceptable for several reasons. First, as I wrote, our students were every bit as capable as any others and our staff worked just as hard and was just as competent as any other staff. Next, one of my core beliefs about public school is that every student who starts must complete (graduate) their compulsory education. We were not hitting that mark. Graduation is the bare minimum and we were falling short with more than one in ten of the students we started with.

To help remedy this, the first thing I communicated with my staff was that it was our mission for every student who started at our high school to graduate. Every person associated with the school was to do everything within their roles and responsibilities to facilitate and lead all of our students to graduation day. Further, we needed to each ensure we were providing the level of service which would lead nothing to chance. We also needed to identify the students who might struggle and determine the supports they would need and provide those resources to them. We also needed to work across departments to coordinate services and our efforts. Most of all, we needed to commit to the types of relationships where teaching and learning could occur and both students and staff understood the goal would not be compromised.

Through this effort I meant to clarify that graduating 100% of our students was our mission. It was not optional, nor subjective in any way. This provided a collective reason for us to work together and one baseline by which we could determine success (many more would follow). Using my Marine leadership experience as my guide, I knew establishing a mission had to come first. I also knew the first and the truest measure of any leader is how fully they accomplish their mission. We did improve our graduation rate at my school through the collective effort of everyone on the staff. More importantly, we were able to accomplish many other great things along the way through the use of a mission accomplishment attitude and the "mission orders" mentality. I'll amplify more on "mission orders" later.

As another example where clarifying the mission worked well, I witnessed a colleague transform an entire student body. While a member of a strong school leadership team, I had a colleague who really saw the value of student

accountability and empowerment. Early on she would insist

we inject students into the solution for nearly every problem

or challenge which came up. I remember her regularly asking

"how can we get students to help us with this?" Or, "Let's get

some students together and ask them for ideas." One of our

core missions became that we would include student input

or participation into every event, activity, or planning

exercise.

It did not take long for us to start seeing the effects

of this brilliant strategy. Almost immediately, students

started taking ownership of their behavior and their learning.

Virtually overnight, discipline issues became less and less,

and school morale was visibly improved. School colors flew

everywhere and spirit days were a blast. My colleague

started a Student Leadership committee and we were

overjoyed when over 100 students showed up for the first

meeting. Our mission as a team now included empowering students and the more we did, the more things improved at our school. Using mission orders, we began transforming our school and our community.

One last thing about mission. It is crucial to the success of the mission that you do not confuse the mission (again the outcomes, products, or the "why" we are doing something) with the process. Let me amplify. We have all learned that goals should be "measurable". Unfortunately, in our field we often see things like meetings or meeting notes as evidence of having accomplished something. Was the mission of the leader, team, or committee to have meetings? If having meetings was the goal, this does not seem very rigorous! If one of your personal goals was to be sure and have meetings with your team every month and take notes then- check! Otherwise, meetings and notes are not really evidence of having accomplished much more than just a meeting. Can you imagine your "why" being "to have more meetings"? Processes are not products and your mission must be based on producing, improving, or changing something tangible not just doing something.

A Bit about Mission Statements

Before moving on, I want to take just a bit of time to write about mission statements. Mission statements, along with other written definitions and written pledges like strategic plans and vision statements are common and usually necessary in many organizations. While mission statements, vision statements, and strategic plans, are all very different things, the point of this section is the same. It is good for the stakeholders to come to a consensus on what exactly we do and what it looks like when we see it. These statements, sometimes voluminous, can serve to give everyone in the organization clear guidance for school and district operations and help subordinate organizations craft their own mission and vision. There are some things for which to be careful however.

A cursory review of various school and district mission statements finds phrases like "college and career readiness", "21st Century Learners (ing)", "Academic Excellence", and "Life-long Learning" among others. Words and phrases like these are great and can serve a purpose. Unfortunately, often much attention is spent wordsmithing the perfect strategic plan, mission, or vision statement while little time is spent actually clarifying the evidence which will show those conditions were met. In other words, if our mission is to produce "life-long learners", what will the evidence be that we have done it? Often these words are published, signs are made, and web sites crafted, but the people charged with carrying them out do not know what the phrasing means or how their role in the organizations contributes to mission success. Worse is when we put these phrases into our missions, visions, and plans and do not build our culture, curriculum, and practices around expected and clearly defined outcomes.

Like the mission of the Marine rifle squad, mission statements need to be very clear on what the expected outcomes are and what they look like when accomplished. Then, it is important we use these mission statements as guides to crafting what we do at every level. If our intent is to produce "life-long learners", how does every program, curriculum, and practice in the district promote and contribute to that end? This needs to be thought of in every planning session and decision making event. Remember that a whole staff working at attaining the same outcome no matter the school, grade level, specialty, or content, is exponentially more powerful than a bunch of individuals working singularly.

Finally, the best mission statements, vision statements, or strategic plans should be summarized into very concise statements so every person in the organization knows what they are without thinking. One idea to do this is to paraphrase or summarize what it is you want every employee in the organization to know and do. Then, write it down or print the text on something no bigger than an index card (credit card is preferred). Finally, laminate the card and encourage every employee to carry the card with their service badge and refer to it until they know it by heart. If we want our organization to accomplish great things, everyone needs to know exactly what those great things are, what the outcome looks like, and how their role or job contributes to them. Just imagine a goal, any goal. Now imagine every person in the organization working together to accomplish the same goal.

I'll close this with one final story. As a Marine Staff Sergeant on my second tour in Japan I was put in charge of forming a team to compete in a "tug-of-war" tournament against local Japanese teams at a neighborhood festival. I surveyed my roster of potential athletes and selected a group of all young, all burley, and all extremely strong and fit Marines to go to the festival and cake-walk through the tournament. When we got to the tournament and lined up against our first opponent we observed the team lining up against us were mostly small, middle-aged men. None were in athletic gear and some even wearing dress shoes! This was going to be easier than we thought.

Well this would not be a good story unless I told you how badly this team of middle aged, smallish Japanese men took about ten seconds to pull my team of physically fit, world-class United States Marines across the line, and that's exactly what happened. The Japanese team all pulled at the same time, in perfect sync, while my Marines flailed about, each trying to use their individual strength to overcome the group of about a dozen other men. One on one, every one of my Marines was much stronger and more athletic, but when the Japanese men all pulled together, we never had a chance. Imagine if you can get everyone at your school or organization on the same end of the rope pulling at the same time?

Mission Type Orders

This leads me to go back and explain a bit more about the idea of "mission orders" or "mission type orders" and why they are effective. In short, the mission type order is a directive given by the leader which simply defines the outcome for the subordinate. How the subordinate accomplishes the mission is up to them. In the military, this is done because the person on the ground, in the fight, is the most informed about the tactical decision and can make the best decision how to deploy his or her people to accomplish the mission. In the case of Chesty Puller, he might not have ordered his fighting withdrawal if he had to clear it with his boss. This is one reason example of why mission orders can be so effective.

While I do not want to infer or compare anything to the seriousness and weightiness of actual combat, the point is if military commanders rely on mission type orders in the most important and dangerous of circumstances when the stakes could not be higher, it is because mission type orders are effective. This style of leadership works and leads to getting things done (I will caveat this point with the fact that military doctrine suggests limiting the amount of mission type orders for when the situation allows). Nevertheless, the overall concept of giving less details about the "how" and more details about the "why", align very well with Sinek's earlier proposition mentioned about the "why" and its necessity to promote full functionality of the brain.

Mission type orders can be applied in non-military, non-combat scenarios with success though. In fact, these types of directives are especially necessary for complex organizations where the leader might not know exactly how his subordinates gets his or her job done. Information Technology (I.T.) is a perfect example. Most of us have no idea how to keep our networks up and running in the organizations in which we work. I am sure this is the case for many of even the biggest bosses. We simply rely on our I.T. people to keep us connected. It would be ridiculous for me, for example, to tell my Director of I.T. how to deploy several thousand laptops. I simply tell him it needs to be done. This is an example of a mission type order.

Similarly, for those of us who work in schools, school leaders cannot be expected to be masters of every area within their purview. I mean principals already have to have a

grasp for running organizations with sometimes hundreds of

people, multi-million dollar budgets, supplies, and an

inventory which includes everything from pencils to fuel oil.

Now imagine being experts in contents ranging from Special

Education to Dance, Theater to English as a Second

Language, Vocational Instruction, and an unlimited and

unending list of other topics.

School leaders have to rely on the teacher experts to

get their jobs done and transfer the knowledge required by

the curriculum to the students and assess their own

effectiveness. As instructional leaders in schools, we can

know all of the best teaching methods and can be experts in

leadership and instruction, but we cannot possibly know

what works best in every grade, content, or discipline.

Whether we know it or not, we are relying on mission type

orders to get the job done. If not, we are not being the most effective leader we can be.

Troop Welfare- Taking Care of People

The second indicator of effective leadership for Marines is called "troop welfare". In the civilian world, this just means taking care of people. While mission accomplishment will always supersede troop welfare, most times there is no way to accomplish the mission if we are not taking care of our people. Sometimes this creates a conundrum for leaders who struggle to find that balance between the two. Make no mistake though, the mission must always be accomplished and the people taken care of.

In the military, our soldiers, sailors, airmen, and Marines are far more committed and obligated to the contracts they sign than the majority of our employees. In fact, they are not only duty-bound, they are committed by law to follow instructions and can be tried and punished for not doing so. The commitment of most employees in the

civilian sector is far less binding, but many jobs could be

considered just as important as our brothers and sisters in

arms.

Unlike in civilian life though, military leaders truly

have an impact on every aspect of the lives of their people.

An example of this is illustrated in one of my favorite movies,

Heartbreak Ridge with Clint Eastwood. In the movie,

Eastwood plays the part of a throwback Gunnery Sergeant

assigned to a rag-tag bunch of Marines led by a well-meaning

but very green, inexperienced second lieutenant. One of

Eastwood's Marines takes an unauthorized absence (UA- or

more commonly known as AWOL) which means he was not

at his appointed place of duty. In a chaotic scene, Highway

drives out to a trailer park to find the missing Marine has

taken on another job to meet the needs of his family

consisting of a young wife and several children. In his

typically gruff but caring style, Highway hands the wife a

handful of money, chews out the Marine, and makes him

return to the base. Highway intervened directly to save the

young man from not only being charged with a violation, but

also helped his family and got the Marine back in good

standing.

The best military leaders know everything about

their people and support their every need. This includes big

things like career advice, personnel evaluations, and pay. It

also includes small things like making sure they go to the

dentist. Military leaders need to be sure their people are

taken care of so they inspect their peoples' rooms and

council them on their hygiene. They check to ensure things

like their car insurance and registration are up to date and

they give them safety briefs on the weekends and before

they go on leave. Imagine trying to do some of these things

with the people you lead!

Everyone Needs to be Supported

Although we do not have the reach of military leaders, we can still take care of our people. Usually in the education field this comes in the form of "support". I put this word in quotes because we use it so often in our field, I am not sure we even have it defined. If you are like me you have probably often read things like "all students can succeed with the right support", or heard from a teacher "I just don't feel supported". Often these statements are made without evidence because we use the word support to mean so many things it really equates to everything and nothing. Nevertheless, both of these statements can be true and we need to examine how taking care of people and "support" are essentially the same things.

All Students can Succeed with the Right Support

Fact check: TRUE! All human beings are organically intelligent beings. God made us last and when He was finished He assessed his greatest creation as "very good" (He

assessed everything else He made only as "good"). This

means we are that much better than any other creation here

on earth! He created us to be infinitely more intelligent than

even the second most intelligent creation and then put us in

charge over everything on earth. He did not do this just for

some of us either. God made every one of us intelligent.

Every single one.

The evidence is all around us. We all know of

students who can sit home for hours mastering a complex

video game, or pass the hunter safety course, but cannot

write a five paragraph essay. I am sure most of us have also

met the student athlete who masters his coach's complex

offense or defense but still struggles to pass the state math

assessment. Some of us may even know the student who can

hold down a job, raise a baby, take care of her brothers and

sisters, and pay the bills for her drug-addicted mother, but cannot complete her homework. I would contend the evidence is everywhere which says each of these students in innately intelligent, can learn, and has what it takes to succeed at the highest levels of our school system.

Each student listed in the examples above needs the right support to mitigate whatever obstacle is standing in the way of his or her efficacy. Sometimes, providing the support is difficult because we do not have the direct oversight like the military leaders. We cannot just walk in and physically rescue every student from their difficult circumstances (even though we want to and many of us do it when and where we can). Other times, we may not have the skills or resources or don't know how to reach the student. This is often the case with the student who is highly motivated about everything except school. Unfortunately, and in the most-rare circumstances, we just choose not to provide the support the student needs. We either have too much on our plate, too many students with high needs, or just do not care enough.

Since this book is strictly about leadership, I have to limit my discussion on how we help our students with the highest needs. Volumes can and have been written about this subject and while I have my own thoughts on this, I am far less qualified than many others to write about it. There are two recommendations I can make from my own experience to better support our students with the most challenging circumstances and they are somewhat related. I will leave out the obvious which is including the parents in this process. A school/parent relationship and partnership are vital to making anything happen in any school so I will state that as evident.

After ensuring the parent is on the team, the next suggestion goes back to knowing our mission and being willing to reach across our school or organization to help every student. Collaborating horizontally and vertically

across our school and school district gets us out of our silo

and gains allies in our efforts to help. We all have access to

guidance counselors, the school nurses, special education

coordinators, reading specialists, librarians, and other

administrators. If all of us in the school and district

understand our mission and are committed to its

accomplishment, we will all get involved. We will all care

enough to reach as many students as possible and the

synergy of all parties working towards the same end will

increase each of our effectiveness.

As a young school leader, I made the common

mistake believing that my team and I could fix everything

ourselves. Sometimes, I even resented outsiders from the

district office who I saw as wanting to interfere in our

operations or even selfishly usurp my authority. As I gained

wisdom though, I saw the educators from outside of our

school were just people like us who wanted to help students learn (and the district was paying them a lot of money to do so). Many were incredible resources on which I was denying my own students and losing out to other schools. After several years as a school leader I made the commitment that no resource would go untapped and took advantage of everything I could to support every student.

Next, I find that we often forget about the many organizations and people outside our schools who are lined up to help and just don't know what to do. Aside from the many charitable organizations, parent organizations like PTA, PTO, or Boosters, faith-based groups, and proprietary organizations are ready and willing to provide people and resources to our schools. There are entrepreneurs, clubs, veteran's organizations, and professional sports teams. The list is endless. The trick is to not limit yourself or remain closed to opportunities which might pop-up and be ready to take advantage of them. I firmly believe that never before

has it been more important to recruit and include every

member of the community to help our children and improve

our schools.

What Really is Support?

To be fully transparent, coming from the military

community I still have a bit of trouble empathizing with the

statement "I just don't feel supported", but it is something

we have to take very seriously when we hear it. Sometimes I

think this phrase really means "I don't like what you are

doing as the school/district leader" or "I don't agree with this

decision", or, "I have done it this way forever, I am not

changing now", or finally "that is not how the last

school/district leader did things". In an unhealthy

environment, cries for support are often masks for low

morale or for those who are unhappy or disagree with the

direction of the organization. Using the term "support" can

be a way to extort the leadership to comply with their own

selfish desires knowing the last thing school leaders want is

the reputation of not being supportive. If your organization

sounds like this, you are in the right place.

Providing Tangible Support for Educators

I remember clearly my first year as a school leader. I

checked into my new school and was welcomed by a great

group of administrators. We hung out all summer making

plans for the coming year and while I had no idea about most

of what we spoke, I knew it was going to be a great year. All

summer they reassured me to not worry, they would be

there backing me up and taking care of me until I got my feet

under me. Then came the first day of school.

The buses dropped off the students and I remember

feeling very small as over a thousand students poured

through the front door towards me at the same time. We

got them into first period and I retired to my office for about a minute before the radio started to explode with requests for help. "I need an administrator to 331", came the first call. "I need an administrator to 214" came another. "Administrator in the basement asap!" sounded someone in obvious need of help. My fellow administrators who promised to have my back were gone. Out the door they went, without me that day, and for the remainder of the year. I am pretty sure what they thought and what I thought *having someone's back* meant were not exactly the same thing.

I relay this story not because those leaders were not doing the best possible job they could do. They were doing what they thought was right and this is probably how they were trained. You know "Sink or swim. He is an administrator now, he needs to step it up". Much of that is true. If you are going to step into school leadership, you better be ready. Nor do I share that story not to show my colleagues or school in a bad light. The school and my colleagues are generally top performers. I relay this story because this is exactly how not to look out for a subordinate and their welfare!

No matter that I was promoted and should have known how to handle new and stressful situations, I was a stepping up into something entirely different than I was used to. Good leadership means employing your people within their capabilities and supporting them along the way. My colleagues (most of whom have moved up the school leadership chain and with who I am still close) did what they had always done- put out fires. Unfortunately, I learned, this was the preferred method of operations at this school and we were always moving from fire to fire.

So how can we take care of your people (troop welfare) and really provide the tangible support they need to do their jobs? Frankly, the concept of taking care of your people does not change as a true leadership indicator no matter your business. Educators differ a bit because we are

information builders, and unlike other industries, information

builders need to feel empowered and responsible in order to

self-actualize and be most effective. In the absence of this

empowerment, many educators can become cynical,

negative, and unmotivated. Schools or districts with these

type of personnel will have problems with morale which are

indicated by things like high turnover or absenteeism.

Therefore, I have listed several things we can do as

educational leaders to take care of or support our "troops":

1) **Maslow Matters for Teachers too**- If we have

been in education for any time at all we know we

cannot reach the top of Maslow's hierarchy of

needs if we don't meet the needs at the bottom

of the pyramid first. This is the same for

teachers. We must ensure teachers physical and

mental needs are being met. Do they know how

to access their pay stub, health-care, or

Employee Assistance? Do they know how to find

an apartment near school? Is everything going

Ok with them personally? New teachers should

be connected with a mentor or sponsor to help

them with everything they need coming to the

school or district. Everyone needs to feel like

they can rely on any of the leaders in an

organization to help them with anything from a

late night flat tire to helping them find a text

book for a graduate course.

2) **Keep them informed**- This one is huge. Teachers

need to be informed. They need to understand

what we are doing, when, and why. They are

typically meticulous planners so they want to

understand what is coming and how they can

prepare. The most important thing we can do

with teachers is communicate proactively and effectively.

3) **Listen**- Another important thing we can do to take care of our educators is to listen. We do this for a couple of reasons. First, our teachers are super-smart, caring, and often have great suggestions. Next, teachers need to feel in control and like most of us, when others listen to us, we are validated as professionals and confirmed as contributing members of the team. Those of us in the information building profession need this to be productive.

4) **Just say YES!** There is never a good reason to say "no" to something without a good reason. The excuse of "if I say yes to this person, I'll have to say yes to everyone" is usually a fear not realized. I try to be agreeable with staff

whenever possible unless there is a good reason

and when there is a good reason to say no,

simply communicate the reason honestly.

5) **Train and Equip them properly-** If we were to

think of the teaching world like an Air Force, the

teachers would be the pilots. Each of the rest of

us in the organization has one goal and that is to

keep those planes in the air. In other words, we

need to resolve every challenge, hurdle, and

problem so they can continue to teach

effectively. We need to be sure they have

received the training and resources they need to

teach the classes they are assigned. They need

working technology, up to date material, and

functioning equipment like desks and filing

cabinets. We need to provide them coaching

and mentoring, form effective teams, take care

of covering their classes when they are ill or have

an emergency, and give them solid actionable

feedback so they can become better teachers.

More than anything, we need to provide the type

of environment free from distractions so they

can engage in their craft and take care of the

students.

Summing things up

Every person can be a leader and improve their

leadership abilities. Most leaders are not born, they develop

through training and personal experience. The two indicators

of leadership are mission accomplishment and troop welfare.

Mission accomplishment always outweighs troop welfare in

terms of importance, but the mission cannot usually be

accomplished without the people being taken care of

effectively. This often creates a conundrum for leaders who

have to balance their resources to take care of their people while keeping the mission at the forefront of everyone's activity. The mission can be compared to an organizations "why". Getting everyone in the organization to commit to the same "why" is exponentially more powerful than everyone pursuing their own "why".

Putting this in to Practice

Reflection Question: How will your leadership change knowing the two most important indicators of leadership are mission accomplishment and taking care of people- in that order?

Suggestions for Action: Create a mission statement for one of your current leadership roles. Think about your position as a school or district leader, committee leader, parent, or coach. What will your leadership cause for the team you are leading to accomplish or complete?

CHAPTER 3

Common Traits of Good Leaders

The list of traits and characteristics of good leaders is probably exhausting and non-exclusive. In most cases we will find some leaders lead with an abundance of similar characteristics while others are limited to just few on which they rely heavily. In other words, every good leader probably possesses certain characteristics others do not and vice versa. The Marines list 14 different leadership traits which, like everything else, they infuse into the core of every Marine. I have added humility to the list because I believe the best leaders are humble and allow for input and feedback. The fifteen leadership traits I discuss further here are:

Justice	Judgement	Decisiveness	Dependability
Tact	Initiative	Endurance	Bearing
Courage	Knowledge	Loyalty	Enthusiasm
Integrity	Unselfishness	Humility	

I will offer my own quick interpretation of each of these traits and why they can be applied to any leadership situation.

Justice- When someone has been given power over another person, they have a tremendous responsibility to exercise the authority commensurately. Justice not only equates to meeting every stakeholder's needs regardless of circumstances beyond their control, it extends beyond words like fairness. Fairness, while important can often be interpreted to mean "the same" and we are learning more and more that "the same" is not always fair or just.

Leaders should be able to interpret the totality of circumstances to make just, fair, and impartial decisions about the people and circumstances over which they have charge. Justice does not always mean every person gets exactly the same thing. After all, if we believe in differentiated instruction, then what every student gets in terms of time, resources, and energy will differ based on their individual needs. Being just means applying your leadership with regard to these needs and ensuring every student's or stakeholder's needs are being met to the best of your ability. Just getting what everyone else gets is not justice.

The term justice comes up a lot when discussing school discipline. It is being increasingly suggested school discipline procedures and protocols have not been just resulting in higher volumes of exclusion of students from certain sub-groups. This is a complex issue, and while I believe there is something to the fact that African American males, for example, make up a small percentage of the overall population of students but represent a statistically larger percentage of out of school suspensions, I believe this phenomenon requires a lot of attention and action. It does not mean however, putting school districts on watch lists or taking away funding when they do not meet arbitrary outcome targets. Unfortunately, systems at every level have a bad habit of making sweeping decisions on the basis of only one type of data which will drive only surface changes. Justice really means examining a whole problem and applying to the situation what is needed.

I write all of this to say that justice is the trait at the heart of this problem and many others. Things like discipline matrixes and "progressive discipline" have been adopted because they appear to be "fair". Well as I have already written, fairness is not justice, and when we equate decisions about behavior to a matrix or checklist we end up with quantitative data we do not like. Worse, students are not treated in a just manner nor getting the type of support they need. School discipline must have at it's core the mission of supporting all student's needs in order to help them succeed and grow. Any other outcome is not justice.

Judgement- One of the quickest ways to soil your reputation as a leader is to be perceived as having bad judgement. This is particularly more important the higher up a leader advances. Good leaders are able to size up conditions, weigh evidence, and make decisions which will have the greatest opportunity to succeed. Fortunately, education is one industry where we typically have time to collect data and make sound decisions. We also have scores of good people around us with whom we can collaborate and a myriad of resources and doctrine to which we can refer to help us make sound decisions. There is really no excuse for poor judgement in the education industry. One example of how I learned to increase my skills with judgement comes from my friend and mentor. This is the leader who first encouraged me and got me into school leadership.

Leading a top school as the lead learner for well over a decade, my friend and colleague Rick has forgotten more about education than most of us know. Shortly after becoming an administrator, I was home one evening and Rick gave me a call (I'll paraphrase), "Hey Steve, I have this thing happening at my school and I wanted your input on what I should do". My first thought was "why the heck are you asking me? You know more than I will probably ever know". I refrained from saying that aloud, listened to his issue, and offered my input. The reason I tell this story is if Rick can ask a green, unknowing new administrator for feedback on an issue at his school, we should all be looking for feedback. I have rarely made decisions since that day without soliciting input or collecting data. Getting feedback and collecting data help us make those good decisions and improve our judgement.

Decisiveness- While it is rare we have to make snap decisions, we cannot be afraid to make them when necessary. This is particularly true when it comes to safety or student welfare. It is always better to weigh in on the side of safety. When we have the time to collect information, we cannot let the process of collecting data and soliciting feedback inhibit our willingness to make hard decisions. We also need to be careful not to waffle once we have made decisions. This is not to say a good leader cannot change his or her mind, sometimes it makes sense to do so. Just remember a famous leader once said, "Let your yes mean yes and your no mean no".

Unfortunately, school and district leaders often have to wait on others before they can decide. In the case where you need approval from higher echelons of leadership like the superintendent or school board, it is important leaders do not let this stifle decisions. The leader needs to be respectfully assertive and can gain the answer they need and then make the call. Like the song goes, "If you choose not to decide, you still have made a choice".

Sticking to policy and predetermined, or existing practice is always a good place to start when evaluating a decision. Even though I will argue we should always question "the way we have always done it", I am talking more about solid, written practices which until rewritten need to be followed. Written doctrine such as school district policy or code cannot be ignored and, in some cases, are illegal to ignore. Often leaders can use precedence or policy to make their decision much easier.

Dependability- Leaders need to say what they mean and do what they say. If you tell a student you will be at his or her game, you need to be there. If a student in the hall wants to meet with you later, meet with him or her. Return phone calls and follow through on even the smallest detail. Leaders become great when they can be relied upon to do what they say they will do.

This is especially true with your stakeholders who will often only gauge their judgement of your effectiveness as a leader based on their limited, direct experience with you. Returning phone calls from community members and parents and listening intently to their concerns can go a long way in solidifying your reputation as a dependable caring leader. Following through with what you say to stakeholders is critical. No one wants to hear at a Board Meeting, "I spoke to the principal who said she would take care of it but I never heard from her again". Avoid this by doing what you say and then following up to close the loop with the stakeholder. This is not just for parents or other community members either.

Students and especially teachers need to feel like if you say something, you can be depended on to follow through.

Integrity- Every Marine knows the answer to the question "what is the most important leadership trait?" It is Integrity. This is true in every industry, under every condition. When I first started in administration, I noticed some leaders had the habit of telling "white lies" or partial truths, especially to parents who were not always fully aware of what goes on in classrooms or schools. One famous excuse is "we cannot share that with you because of privacy". Sometimes this is true, but not always. Another partial truth is, "it's just not in the budget" when in fact many schools have excess funds at the end of every school year they are scrambling to get rid of.

I refused to do this and made it clear to our team we would never be less than honest with everyone with whom we came in contact. This included student and staff investigations where it was common practice to mislead those being investigated by using phrases like "we heard

from a teacher" or "we received a complaint from a parent"

when that in fact it was not the case. There is just no

substitute for integrity and taking ownership of even the bad

things.

Once people with whom you work think you are not

being fully honest with them it is impossible to change their

mind. I know it is like this for me. Let me tell you a quick

story about something that really solidified my thinking on

this. One of my former supervisors called me up one

afternoon and told me she had been getting a lot of

complaints about something. What she did not know was the

"something" which so many people were allegedly

complaining about effected very few people under my charge

and I knew each one of them. I also knew one of those

people was very close to my supervisor and was strongly

against my direction. It was obvious that my supervisor had

not been getting "a lot of complaints". She was getting a

complaint from one person who had no real basis to

complain about the new policy anyways. My supervisor was

taking the full account from her colleague and then validating

her inquiry to me on false pretenses. Suffice to say, my

opinion of that supervisor has changed permanently because

I know she was not fully honest with me during that

exchange.

Endurance- Teaching is hard. School leader and Author

Jimmy Casas wrote that we expect teachers to cram "one

year of work into nine months and do it with the care and

compassion of a surrogate parent" (Casas, 2017). It is both

physically and emotionally taxing. In many ways school

leadership is even harder. Our best leaders arrive long before

the first bell and work well into the night. High school

administrators are particularly challenged with full slates of

year-round sports, concerts, plays, and community events all which require coverage and most of which the principal is

expected to personally attend. As a school leader, my family

had dinner together in my office often several times a week

and it was not uncommon for someone to find my daughter

doing her homework at my office table after school. The

point of this is not to suggest I worked any harder than

anybody else, it is just to remind us how demanding our jobs

are and how ready we need to be to put in that level of work.

To lead, we need to be physically fit, and mentally ready to

endure conditions greater than those we are leading.

One area in which good leaders need high volumes of

endurance (and later bearing) is in the need for an unending

supply of patience. We have to remember that the onus is on

us (pun intended) to be the ones who have to endure the

angry parents, the unreasonable teacher, or the student we

have spoken to one million times about the same thing. A

wise leader once taught me that most of the people we work

with as school and district leaders do not have the benefit of the education or training we have had nor do they have the insight to things like school operations, policy, and school law. We are school leaders for a reason and having a high capacity for endurance allows us to tactfully navigate the challenges other people are just not required or able to navigate.

Bearing- To me, bearing is the word which kind of means "never let them see you sweat". One way to quickly get a Marine in check is to tell him or her "not to lose their bearing". In short, we do not wear our emotions on our sleeve, we do not lose our temper, and we do not let others decide for us the behavior we choose to exhibit. This is such a difficult trait for new leaders to get used to because it takes a combination or grace and humility. For me, I had to learn this the hard way coming from a system where I was instantly followed as a leader.

In my early days as a school leader (and some of my weaker days as an experienced school leader) I could became visibly frustrated at times when someone was blatantly disrespectful (especially parents or other adults). I engaged in arguments and made sure I won them. I had to learn and remind myself often that I was the one with the training, and education, and my position expected and demanded I have the patience and temperament to deal with angry parents or employees. That is why I was given the job!

Tact- Tact is the ability to have a hard conversation without creating hard feelings. Most of the people I work with have advanced degrees and they are very good at what they do. It is critical we maintain a respectful dialogue with them even when correcting or redirecting them. I had a great boss once whose strategy for correcting me was to just ask questions. By the end of the conversation I had revealed to myself where I screwed up and how I could do better next time. She rarely had to tell me anything because I was doing all the

work telling myself.

Having a lack of tact can really sour relationships, and

relationships are central to every leader's effectiveness.

Relying on excuses like "Oh that is just him, don't take

offense", or "you know her, she has no filter" are really just

weak excuses for selfish and unprofessional behavior. This is

not to say we have not been guilty of being less than tactful

in stressful situations or moments of weakness, but chalking

up disrespectful or hostile work behavior to someone's self-

entitlement to be rude is unacceptable. Being tactful means

leading and modeling with civil discourse. This will help

promote positive behavior across your organization and have

a positive impact on culture and relationships.

Initiative- Doing what needs to be done without being told or

directed. Great leaders often get to high positions because

they are doing what needs to be done before anyone else.

Every great invention, business, and innovation were started

by someone who saw something needed to be done or

created and acted. As leaders move up, even more initiative

is needed because there are less and less people telling you

what to do.

One of the many new and difficult things about being

the school or district leader is you have always been the

person with the ideas and the person who then puts them

into practice. School and district leaders just do not have the

time to both think of and implement new practices or ideas.

They still have the ideas, but they have to rely on their team

to develop and implement them. Where the leader must

evolve is in being able to clearly articulate their vision for

their own initiative so someone else can actually implement

the idea.

Unselfishness- Jon Gordon is one of my favorite authors and

talks about "we before me" in his book *The Power of the*

Positive Team (Gordon, 2018). Jon recounts the story of growing up watching his Dad, a New York City Police Officer interact with his partner and how they put each other first. Former Hall of Fame Football player Gale Sayers puts himself third (1st- God, 2nd- friends and family, 3rd- himself), (Sayers & Silverman, 1970). Marines do not even put themselves in the top three, instead listing "God, Country, and Corps" before themselves. The point is, leaders often need to put the needs of others before themselves to accomplish their mission and take care of their people. An example of this is when we give our subordinates credit for everything which goes right and take the blame and ownership for everything which goes wrong. We need to unselfishly publicly praise our staff and patiently and privately mentor and correct them when needed.

In another great book, *Leaders Eat Last*, author Simon Sinek uses an every-day example of Marine leadership as a model for unselfishness. Simon writes that in the Marine Corps, when Marines line up to eat, the senior members of the group automatically take their position at the back of the line. Junior Marines eat first and the leadership eats last, just like in the title. If portions of or even all the food runs out (which happens from time to time), the leaders do not eat, or they eat whatever is left. This is one way Marine leaders demonstrate unselfishness and something which extends beyond just extensions of courtesy to one or two people. The senior Marines will not eat until they are sure every junior Marine has been through the chow line.

Courage- While we are not serving on the battlefield and would not dare to compare the type of courage our nation's warriors have to anything else, being a leader anywhere requires a high level of moral and mental courage. Anyone who has broken up a fight in the cafeteria also knows sometimes it even requires a bit of physical courage. Making those phone calls with our most difficult parents, having conversations with difficult staff, letting people go, telling people you have chosen someone else for a job, engaging students who are making bad choices, and telling your boss he or she is making a bad decision, all require courage and we are all called on to show courage regularly. Our best leaders show courage.

Knowledge- Great leaders need a strong base of knowledge about a myriad of things. One thing my team will tell you I often say is "nobody wants a knucklehead for a boss". This is so true! Most of us want to look up to our leader and believe he or she is not only an expert in our field, but an expert leader. While leaders do not need to be an expert in every field, they need to be an expert at something. Of course, this requires leaders to expand beyond their direct area of expertise and learn about many other things.

Before I became a school administrator, I was a Naval Science teacher for the Naval Junior Reserve Officer Training (NJROTC) program and I was darn good at it. Put me in a chemistry class though, and I probably know less than any student in there. Even though school leaders cannot be expected to be experts in everyone else's profession, they must have a foundational understanding of everyone's job and how they contribute to the mission. In addition to this, if you are a school principal, you also need to know about everything from finance to playing field maintenance, from contract law to ventilation, and virtually everything in between.

Most leaders who are promoted are not ready to step in and do their jobs exceptionally well. They just do not know enough about their role as a new leader yet. This is not to say many new leaders do not step up in responsibility and do great, it just means they are probably even greater after several years in their post. Every leader though, needs to bring a high level of knowledge to the table about their role and about their industry so they can quickly adapt and make the transition into their new role. They still have to effectively lead while they learn.

Loyalty- Similar to commitment, loyalty suggests an allegiance to something or someone. Leaders need a high degree of loyalty to their mission, their team, and their organization. They also need high levels of loyalty to their faith, their families, and themselves. In the same way leaders need to be unselfish, they need to be loyal so their efforts remain focused on those they lead. Of course, in education our first and most unwavering loyalty is to doing what is best for the children 100% of the time.

Loyalty cannot be excluded to the leader's direct interest only. The leader's loyalty also needs to extend to both the parallel and higher echelons of the organization. If the leader is a school leader, they not only need to align their

loyalties with the interests of the district and the state, but

even fellow school leaders within the district and state.

Similarly, the superintendent needs to be aware of

neighboring districts, the state, and United States

Department of Education.

At one point in my career I found myself at three

different rival high schools in three years because I moved

relatively fast through the leadership ladder. Each time I

moved up, I shed one school's colors and instantly became

loyal to my new school and new staff. Changing colors did

not mean completely abandoning my old loyalties, nor did it

mean abandoning my first loyalty to students regardless of

the school they attended. I remained faithful to my friends

and colleagues along the way because leaders also depend

on the relationships they form and depend on them even

after their direct working relationship is over.

This is not to mean that leaders serve to agree with

every policy or thought from higher headquarters, or

sacrifice the interests of their own school or district in favor

of another. As I stated at the beginning of this section, we

should never compromise on our first loyalty which is doing

best for all students. Sometimes, because this is our first

loyalty, we need to confront things to protect that interest.

Whether it is bad policy or decisions which we know will

adversely affect the quality of a free and appropriate public

education, we are morally and professionally obligated to

stand up and be loyal to our students. Finally, when it comes

to accomplishing the mission, it takes a team, and you need

your team just as loyal to the success of every student and

this starts with your personal example.

Enthusiasm- This can be described as being excited,

interested, and joyful. The best leaders are consciously and

explicitly enthusiastic about their jobs, mainly because they love their jobs and naturally share their feelings with those around them. This does not mean leaders are fake or disingenuous. Real leaders truly enjoy what they do and choose to share it.

I was speaking with a High School Band Director recently and telling him how impressed I was that band teachers can be so motivated about their jobs. I also explained how impressive it was and how difficult it must be to be able to master and teach so many instruments. Our conversation ended with him saying "it's hard, but I have the best job in the world". I agreed aloud, but in my heart, I knew he was wrong because I had the best job in the world. Enthusiasm inspires others around you and reminds them why they got into their job in the first place.

Besides, who wants to go to work every day and not be excited about it? If we are fortunate, we spend over half of our lives working. It just makes no sense not to be excited about something which has that big of an impact on our quality of life. This is good reason enough to be enthusiastic about our jobs, but from a leadership perspective, we should want the same level of enthusiasm for what we do from those we lead. We cannot expect enthusiasm from others if we do not show it ourselves.

Humility- Humility for a leader means having the willingness to listen, collaborate, and be open to accepting you don't know everything. When I first broke into leadership, I was impressed by how assertive many of my colleagues were. They always seemed quick to offer a suggestion or give insight to every problem or discussion. Partly because I was new to the field, I got into the habit of just listening and taking notes. Later I would reflect on the notes, often running things by leaders I trusted. What I found was most of the assertiveness my fellow leaders were demonstrating was usually just filibustering about things which were either very obvious and sometimes even inaccurate. I mean if I had a nickel for every time a school leader got up and said something like "this is a very complex problem, but whatever we decide if we keep the kids and families at the forefront of what we decide, we cannot go wrong". I would be a rich man. This grandstanding is usually accompanied by a very long repeat of the problem and the potential solutions all of which are already on the table. The best leaders do not have to be in the spot light because they are humble.

Humble leaders not only know their limitations and are great listeners, they take ownership of their limits and do not try to hide them. I have served with all kinds of leaders. Marines and civilians. Men and women. Quiet, calm, mousy leaders, and anxious, jumpy screamers. The most impressive leaders with whom I have served had the natural ability to command 100% authority and respect without being overbearing or negative. They do not even seem like they are working for the respect they are getting. They say things like "please", "thank you", and "I am sorry". They still recognize your shortcomings but do not highlight them for you in public.

Great leaders approach every problem from the perspective of a novice. What I mean by this is, leaders who look at every situation from the novice perspective are looking to make an honest assessment as if they know nothing about it before deciding. They actively try to see the problem for what it is and are willing to consider different solutions. Good leaders consider facts in context rather than assuming the problem is something they have already seen, already done, or already have an answer for. They listen attentively, and offer suggestions in the form of questions. Lastly, the best leaders have no doubt in their own abilities, but understand someone else might have an idea or bring something to the table of value and they are willing to listen

and learn.

Finally, great leaders are courteous to everyone, all

the time. This is especially true in today's world of

technology and electronic communication. I knew a great

leader once who could be very short and curt with his

subordinates. His typical response to an email was to simply

respond with "yes", or "no". This exercise in brevity can be

misconstrued by the readers of your messages and should be

avoided.

Knowing it is very hard to decipher tone in electronic

communication for example, I try very hard to be overly

enthusiastic and kind when sending electronic messages. I

am sure to always open every e-mail with an appropriate

salutation and close cordially. While I am undoubtedly more

concise with text messages, I still strive not to be

misinterpreted by being extra respectful. I want my

communications to always be a true indicator of my

commitment to relationships and convey that I am an open

team player. I understand everyone is busy, but the best

leaders are never too busy to exercise friendliness and

courtesy. There is more about communication in chapter

five, but in short, effective communication may be the single

most important thing great leaders need to do better than

anything else.

Summing it up

Leaders possess a number of common traits which

make them effective. Some leaders possess more than others

or in different combinations. The Marines have a list of what

they believe are the 14 most important traits of effective

leaders. The 14 traits are justice, judgement, decisiveness,

integrity, dependability, tact, initiative, endurance, bearing,

unselfishness, courage, knowledge, loyalty, and enthusiasm.

Above all the other leadership traits, Marines see integrity as the most important. Leaders do what they say and say what they mean without telling partial truths or white lies. One of the worst things a leader can do is mislead someone. Trust is very easily lost and difficult if not impossible to regain.

While all of the leadership traits listed above are evident in the best leaders, the following five traits represent (in order) the *Leading Made Simple* traits which I believe are most important and serve as a foundation for all good leadership practices: Integrity, knowledge, judgement, dependability, and humility.

Putting this into Practice

Reflection Question(s): How do the list of leadership traits in this chapter align with the traits you may have believed were the most important for effective leadership before you read this chapter? Which traits do you feel help leaders be most effective? Which traits have the least impact on leadership?

Suggestions for Action: Create a simple T chart for yourself.

On one side of the chart, list the leadership traits (Marine Corps or *Leading Made Simple*) you feel strongest with. Then on the other side, list the traits you think you need to work on more.

CHAPTER 4

Principles of Leading

Along with their leadership traits, Marines also follow certain leadership principles. These principles, like the traits, are characteristics or processes most effective leaders adhere to both to lead *and* become better leaders. Also like the traits, leaders exhibit these in varying amounts with some leaders leaning more heavily on some principles and less on others. While I have used the Marines' Leadership principles as a basis for this chapter, I have blended the ideas with personal tips picked up through experience and training.

Setting the example is probably the first thing I think about when I consider a good leadership principle. In the education community we call this modeling. It is far more likely you will get people to do things you are willing to do yourself. In fact, it is just not good to expect people to do something you are not willing to demonstrate for them in practice. This does not mean just because you are willing to go outside and pick up debris in the parking lot you expect everyone else to do this, it just means you are willing to set the highest standards at all times.

The best school leaders are on display constantly so they need to always be on their game. They show up early, greet staff and students at the door when they get to school, smile, and dress immaculately. They value relationships and never give up on anyone. Simply stated, school leaders need to exhibit the best behaviors and attitudes they would want everyone around them to demonstrate. This goes for everything from being a tireless worker to being a lifelong learner. You will really know you are influencing your people when you notice them using your phrases and mimicking the things you do almost subconsciously. Setting a superlative personal example is the first step to becoming a great leader.

Another core tenet, or principle for a good leader is, in addition to leading by personal example, they understand their own strengths and weaknesses and constantly seek self-improvement. To do this leaders need to constantly seek feedback and then figure out how to implement what they have learned. One of my fellow principals had an interesting way of soliciting feedback. At the end of many summary evaluations he would ask the person being evaluated to evaluate him. I am not sure how honest everyone is at that very moment, but I am sure he got feedback from time to time which really helped. This practice also lends to demonstrating humility and your willingness to improve which also models the kind of behavior you want them to demonstrate. There are some great ways to train to become a better leader in Chapter eight.

Another strong leadership principle which also requires us to constantly improve is being technically proficient at our jobs. While I mentioned several times throughout the previous text that while school leaders cannot be experts at everything, they need to be at least good at most things. This requires staying up on the latest developments in both your own field and the field of school leadership. School leaders have a strong grasp of learning theories, instruction, and classroom management. You have to be able to give subordinates actionable feedback and be a credible resource for information. Finally, you need to demonstrate a love of learning and be active with both presenting and attending professional development both in and out of your school or district.

Strong leaders are also active supervisors. Active supervision is different than micromanagement. Supervision does not mean leaning over people's shoulders and correcting everything they do as soon as they do it. Good supervisors follow up and follow through. Leaders make it clear to their employee they know when the task has been completed to fidelity and gives him or her feedback. Often the feedback can be just a simple "thank you". Principled, effective leaders supervise.

The next principle seems like it might contradict the previous, but it really does not. Bear with me. Before I got into school leadership, I did a lot of part-time sports officiating. One of the sports I officiated was basketball and I would attend clinics each summer to get better at my craft. I remember at one clinic a highly respected official told us the key to great officiating was to "see everything and do as little about it as possible".

I think leadership is much the same thing. As leaders, we need to see everything, but our actions need to be calculated so as not to be too much. We never want to ignore bad behavior from anyone we lead, but every mistake does not require the fifty dollar fine and fifty minute lecture.

Finding the balance is challenging because sometimes we think leadership means fixing everything and everyone, but it really does not. Leadership means creating the kinds of conditions in our organizations which allow for everyone in our charge to perform at the highest possible levels in concert with each other. This coordinated engagement of high performance serves to multiply everyone's production so each performs even better together than they could alone. The best leaders under whom I have served always seemed to know when to step in and know both how far to push me and how much to limit me.

Seeing everything and doing as little about it as possible means not creating rules for everything in your organization which can go wrong. To clarify, I do not intend to converge rules with policies. Every school district needs clear and strong official district policies. School districts are essentially bureau-ocracies funded by the tax payers. All organizations which fall into this category need strong

oversight and regulation. What I am referring to are the

small, almost meaningless rules we create because just a few

employees violate them.

Todd Whitaker is one of my favorite educational

leaders and authors. He provides many examples of this in

his books *What Great Teachers Do Differently, and What

Great Principals Do Differently* (Whitaker, 2013). If you have

not read Todd's work, I highly recommend it. One example

he writes about is called "Stop the Thumping!" which he

hilariously recounts the story of a principal so incensed by

kids "thumping" each other, she interrupts the school with

an announcement defining thumping and calling for its end.

Todd describes how, before the announcement was even

finished, entire classes of children went immediately from

learning to practicing some form of thumping at their desks.

The point is, whether it is thumping, tardiness, teachers being in the halls during class changes, or any other practice, probably 90-99% of people are already making the right choices and following the rules written or not. Introducing rules only does one or more of several things. First, it risks alienating everyone who is already following the rules. Next, creating new rules paints the leader into a corner because now they are compelled to enforce them. And last, the non-rule followers will likely just find a way around the rule or hide it from you. This is even worse! Again, the best practice is to see everything and only do what is necessary to create conditions which promote the kinds of behaviors and practices you want and discourages the practices you do not.

Since I started this part of our conversation about sports, I'll take it just one step further. High performing organizations are like a winning sports teams and team building is another critical principle for effective leaders.

Effective leaders not only form great teams, they love being part of them. Why are teams so great to be a part of? Well, winning probably has something to do with it, but if you have ever been on a great team, you know everyone pulls together for the success of the team. Team members are rooting for each other, supporting each other, and sacrificing for each other. This willingness to do these things more often than not results in sums greater than its parts. In other words, groups of people joined together on a great team will always outperform groups of great people just playing together. Another leadership principle for highly effective leaders is to form your people into effective teams.

Right along with team building is the principle of creating a sense of responsibility amongst your people. Great teams and team members have a high sense of responsibility because the leader has demonstrated a commitment for being responsible for them. Effective leaders take full responsibility for everything which goes wrong. This is hard

for many in education to take seriously because we have

such high standards we feel almost insulted when one of our

colleagues does not live up to them. The attitude of "We

want him or her held accountable, not the leader! The leader

was not even there!" seems to be prevalent when a junior

administrator makes a mistake.

This attitude just does not facilitate or build

responsibility, it actually tears it down. Who is going to be

willing to take any risks in an environment where they are

browbeaten for everything that fails? By stepping up and

taking the blame when something does not work out for one

of my people I am telling them they can take chances, and I

have their backs. They in turn will do the very best they can

to keep me out of hot water. I can always have a

conversation with the person if they dropped the ball, but I am going to take ownership of his or her failure as if it was my own.

Conversely, I am going to give my team credit for everything that goes right. Every good idea I have is going to go to them, every great plan, every great suggestion too. Giving your team credit for all the good things reminds them how great it is to do great things. They will return the favor by being creative, looking for ways to continuously improve, and finding ways to be positive and impact the team.

Finally, communication is a critical component of highly effective leadership. Chapter five, later in this book is committed to communication and messaging. What I will say here as a tease to chapter five is that communication is vast and includes not only everything you say but also what you do not say. Never assume something is obvious and be sure your messages are clear enough that anyone can understand them- even if they have no prior knowledge. Keeping your people informed, especially in education, keeps everyone

calm and feeling like you care enough to tell them what is

going on. Being silent makes them uneasy or worse leads

them to believe you are hiding something.

I remember after a few years as a principal, I was told

by someone they heard I was not coming back the next year.

I asked a few of my confidants on the staff if they had heard

anything like that and found out there was a rumor

circulating that I was gone after that year. I was livid! Why

was I being moved after such a short time? I had done what I

thought was a great job to that point and felt like my time

was just beginning. I waited until the end of the day to call

my boss. When we connected, I asked her if it were true.

Was I being moved after that year? "What?" She exclaimed.

"You are just coming into your own. Why would you even

think that?" I told her that a few people on my staff had

been circulating that rumor and she laughed telling me that

was common during this time of year and to get out in front

of it by stepping up my communications about the next

school year to make it clear I was not going anywhere.

Lesson learned! If you do not communicate your own

message, someone else will communicate it for you.

***Leading Made Simple* Principles of Leadership**

Like the leadership traits, the leadership principles

above provide a solid framework for leadership. The most

effective leaders try their best to stick to all of them. Since

this book tried to simplify leadership, I have narrowed down

the above leadership principles to what I feel are most

important:

1) Set the example and model the behaviors and

   practices you wish to see.

2) Always reflect on your own practices and seek ways

   to continuously improve.

3) Know your job and do it well.

4) See everything and only do what is necessary to create the kinds of behaviors and practices you want to see.

5) Practice listening twice as much as speaking.

Summing it up

Like the leadership traits, leadership principles are guides, or framework, for leaders. This framework allows leaders to hone and improve their ability to lead their people. Most effective leaders follow these guides both instinctively and because of their training and experience. The Marine Corps follows eleven leadership principles. The Marine Corps Leadership Principles are (MCIP 6-11B, 2008):

1) Know yourself and seek self-improvement.

2) Be technically and tactically proficient.

3) Know your people and look out for their welfare.

4) Keep your people informed.

5) Set the example.

6) Ensure the task is understood, supervised and

   accomplished.

7) Train your people as a team.

8) Make sound and timely decisions.

9) Develop a sense of responsibility among your

   subordinates.

10) Employ your team in accordance with its capabilities.

11) Seek responsibility and take responsibility for your

   actions.

For the purpose of *Leading Made Simple,* I have reduced the

baseline leadership principles to five and reworded them

slightly:

1) Set the example and model the behaviors and

   practices you wish to see.

2) Always reflect on your own practices and seek ways

   to continuously improve.

3) Know your job and do it well.

4) See everything and only do what is necessary to create the kinds of behaviors and practices you want to see.

5) Practice listening twice as much as speaking.

By reducing the eleven Marine leadership principles to just five, I hope to create a framework which can more easily be remembered and practically applied. I have also changed the language to align more with things we actually say in our field. For example, I took "be technically and tactically proficient" and changed it simply to read "know your job and do it well".

Putting this into Practice

Reflection Question(s): How does having principles of leadership promote our ability to lead?

Suggestions for Action: Compare the eleven Marine Corps leadership principles to the five *Leading Made Simple* principles. Then, try to create a leadership principle on your

own that is not included in either of these two lists.

CHAPTER 5

Communication and Messaging

Unlike any other skill, ability, trait, principle, or custom, the factor which will most effect the authority, followership, reputation, and ability of every leader is his or her ability to communicate. There is just no substitute for effective communication. If we do not communicate our own message accurately, timely, and in the proper tone, someone else will communicate it for us in their own form. That message can easily then become the leader's message regardless of its accuracy. Effective leaders are masters at communication and use communication to influence their stakeholders to willingly follow them. The three areas we will focus on for communication will be communicating broadly with stakeholders (mass communication), interpersonal communications, and communicating with social media.

Mass Communicating with Stakeholders in General

For the purpose of *Leading Made Simple*, I have broken down mass communicating with stakeholders into three groups: communication with the student body, communicating with the staff, communicating with the community as a whole. Each group has its own unique and different nuances in terms of frequency and detail so each will be addressed separately. To be sure you reach as many of your target audience as possible, you probably want to use as many mediums (phone, text, email) as possible.

A couple of general rules of thumb for mass communications is that is needs to be timely and economical. What I mean by this is, too much communication can be just as bad as none at all. Messaging too soon can also be as bad as messaging too late. In other words, if you send out long, detailed messages to your community every Friday, you may risk losing them to fatigue early on. Likewise, if you are giving people a six-week heads up for an event, you cannot expect

them to remember it. Timely and economic messages are

important for effective messaging.

Let me give you an example. My daughter had a

principal once who really wanted to keep the parents

informed. Her Friday phone calls would last ten minutes or

longer. In addition to sending very detailed information

about school operations she liked to recognize staff and

students on the call (all good things to report- on paper). The

problem was, I just did not have the time to listen to her long

messages which contained very little which pertained to me

or my student. Unfortunately, when I would see the school's

number on the caller ID, I sent it right to voicemail and

usually never got around later to listening. In this case,

overcommunicating was just as bad as not communicating at

all.

Another rule for mass communication is that messages need to be concise and brief. This goes along with economy or frequency of messaging. A good order for mass messaging is to start with a salutation ("Good Afternoon Spartan Nation!"), then your message ("I am calling this afternoon to tell you……."), followed by a closure ("I thank you for listening and look forward to seeing you on campus soon"). Be sure to change the format depending on the method of the message going out. In other words, do not just send your phone message out in text. Change up the content to match the method of delivery (Instead of "I am calling you for….", you would write "I am writing to tell you…."). Having a standard format helps you keep your messages cordial and informative and people may even look forward to what news you have for them.

Small things matter in mass communication and can make a huge difference. Be sure to proof read all of your messages or even better, have someone look them over for you. It is just embarrassing to send out a message with a spelling or grammatical error. We are teachers and should not make those kind of mistakes. In another example of mass communication, most schools all have either a manual or automated sign right out front of their buildings. I cringe when I drive by a school or district office and see illiterate, old, or inaccurate information on the front sign. With all the teachers in the building, we have no excuse for poor grammar or spelling in our communications.

Finally, from the perspective of the Central Office, we need to remember our schools are mass communicating with the students, staff, and families already. If a family has students in two or three schools, the messages really start to pile up. The last thing they want is to hear the same information they just got from two different principals and then again from the superintendent or other central office administrator. Therefore, Central Office folks need to be sure

they understand what the schools are sending out and fit

themselves into the communication plan so there are limited

redundancies and no conflicting messages. One final warning

about mass messages, never send out something you do not

mind ending up in the newspaper. Assume any messages you

send out will appear in print so be sure you can stand by

everything you broadcast.

Mass Communicating with Students

School leaders will want to communicate directly

with the student body from time to time. Some principals

recommend addressing the student body more often while

others save their direct communication with students for

when it is really important. This is something only the leader

themselves can determine based on the make-up of the

students and the amount of direct, explicit influence he or

she wants to have on the student body. Some student bodies

will need more direct contact with the principal- especially younger students. Others will only need to be addressed directly by the leader on occasions like during special events, unusual occurrences, or before holiday breaks. Older students usually fall into this category.

Younger students are probably best addressed either through morning or after-school announcements or by sending a note home in their weekly folder or bookbag. If the principal getting on the announcements is infrequent, you can alert the staff you will be making the announcement and they can make a big deal of it with the students. Doing this can get them excited to hear what you have to say. Leaders have to be able to gauge how often to address the children directly. I had a very experienced principal tell me she only addressed the students directly when it was necessary to avoid them tuning her out.

Older students can be addressed through e-mail or other electronic media such as the many proprietary software available through talk or text. Most teenagers prefer to be communicated with in this way and using electronic media will definitely maximize your reach. Be sure to keep communication with students as explicit and brief. As Joe Friday says "Just the facts". Never use this method to try to modify behavior of groups of students. Mass punishment is never good, nor is mass public admonishment. Do this and you might end up seeing reply messages on Instagram with a following of unkind comments.

Mass Communicating with Staff

As I mentioned earlier in this text, teachers generally prefer to know as much as possible. There is almost no risk in telling them too much. There is also no risk in overpraising them which is why it is good to be sure and recognize or praise some or all of the teachers every time you address them as a whole. Communication with staff should be friendly, but not informal- informational, brief, and regular. Done effectively, staff will look forward to your "Friday Memo" or "Oh by The Way". I recommend mass communication is done electronically and in memo or newsletter format. Rarely you might need to do a mass phone call, but these will be irregular. In the event of having to contact staff to inform them of an emergency or tragedy, personal calls should be made. You can enlist the help of your guidance department or fellow leaders if your staff is large or if the message needs to be timely.

Regardless of the format in which I am communicating, I usually start my teacher communications with a friendly salutation like "Greetings Staff! Please let me start by thanking (congratulating, shouting out, etc.…)". Starting each message with an authentic thanks or congratulations helps set a positive tone for the message.

Just remember to be brief and to the point as no one really

has time for long messages. This is another thing which will

help the staff look forward to your message as they will want

to hear about the great things their colleagues are involved

in or doing and you are respectful not to take up more time

than is necessary.

Next, I try to send a bulleted list of items which I

think are important. The list always includes dates and times

of key events or deadlines. I like to use the bulleted format

whenever possible because it helps keep both the writer

(me) and the reader organized. Using bullets also cuts down

on superfluous verbiage helping to keep the message

concise. Sometimes you might include things like birthdays or

other special events, but this depends on how you plan to

have the message perceived. In one school I worked, the

principal's secretary sent out a "Plan of the Week" which

listed all of the events going on at school that week including

birthdays and special events and discipline data for the week.
The message I would send was much more expansive in
scope and more forward looking than the "Plan of the
Week".

I try hard never to allow my weekly messages to drift
into something corrective or reprimanding. I will send
general reminders (Example: "Please remember it is great to
see everyone in the halls during hall exchanges! This is a
great way to form relationships and meet students you do
not know"), but I try hard to avoid being critical (Example:
"Please remember it is our professional responsibility to….").
This is especially true when the majority of the staff is
already doing the right thing. In this case, approach the staff
whose behavior you want to change directly.

I like to close my weekly memo with some kind
words thanking the staff for their continued support and how
I look forward to serving them further. I also like to include

an inspirational quote at the bottom of my memo which usually helps me as much as it does the readers. Doing little things like these helps to set the tone and gives people a look into your mindset about teaching, learning, and leading.

As I stated, there are rare times when you might need to make mass phone calls to the staff and you'll want to do these a bit differently. As stated, you'll never want to send a recorded message with bad news. To share bad news, you will want to do it directly. If your staff is too big or time is of the essence, have the members of your team help. When you are forced to mass call to inform staff about something, the real key is to be as brief as possible and give staff a way to contact you back if they need more information. Everyone can get "message fatigue". If they learn your messages are long and/or unnecessary, they will stop listening to them.

I would like to touch a bit on whole group, face to face meetings which always seem to be received with mixed emotions. Those at the very beginning of the year and the last meeting of the year always seem to be exciting and motivating. Those in the middle often take a lot to get people up for. One thing which has seemed to work with my staff is to be sure I have some of the more positive and "popular" staff members lead portions of the meeting. Always try to do some staff recognition and point out personally some of the great things people are doing in the building. Minimize how much information you give out which you already give out in the weekly memo. There is really no need to repeat what is in your weekly message other than to remind them they are responsible for everything in the weekly memo. Just like having a good relationship with another person, the leader needs to be able to have a strong relationship with the entire staff. Good leaders take advantage of whole group interactions to cultivate and grow that relationship.

Mass Communicating with the School or District Community

Every school and district leader must communicate effectively with the parents and other community stakeholders. Usually these communications take the form of mass phone calls, e-mails, or other electronic media blasts. The best leaders take advantage of face to face opportunities to communicate with their stakeholders knowing this is where you really make deposits into the "relationship bank". Examples of this are attending awards events with partner organizations, sports events, community events, and even faith based events. Similar to the way the best school and district leaders grow their relationships with individual students, staff, and community members, they also grow their relationship with their community as a whole through effective mass communication.

Like your weekly memo with the staff, I recommend the school and/or district leader create some type of community newsletter which is sent out monthly or quarterly. If applicable, you can even print the item and ask local businesses to pass them out or have them available in their stores and offices. These newsletters should be positive, informative and no more than one page front and back. There are many proprietary software available for this, but simple document producing software will work if you are not artsy or techy. The newsletter should include some staff and student recognition, a list of important reminders, and maybe even some fun facts or school trivia. If you are not the creative type, you may want to recruit someone within your organization who is adept with some kind of presentation software to help create your newsletter.

Phone, email, or other electronic blasts are another way to get out short important messages. The same guidelines apply for these as the blasts we send to staff and students. Be clear, be brief, and provide a means for the listener to find more information about the subject (Example: "for more information, please visit our website or give us a ring here at school").

Interpersonal Communications

There are essentially four areas of interpersonal communications: speaking, listening, writing, and non-verbal. For the purpose of this section, I will start with listening. Nothing signals to someone "you are important", "you matter", and "I want to help you" more than active listening. Active listening signals to our audience we are genuinely interested in hearing what the other person is saying, we are processing it, and value it.

While we probably do not want to admit it, we have all likely engaged in an exchange with someone where our only purpose for listening to them is so we can find an opening to speak. This is not listening! Active listening

includes things like eye contact, nodding, asking probing

questions, and acknowledging what your partner speaker is

saying. Some communication gurus will even suggest

paraphrasing what the person said, asking for confirmation,

and then responding. Note-taking can be OK, but if you are

going to take notes during a discussion, it is always a good

idea to ask for permission ("You have a lot of important

things to say which I do not want to miss, is it OK if I take

some notes while we talk?").

Listening does a number of things for us starting with

creating a vehicle for building relationships. Aside from just

sending signals of reverence for the other person, when you

listen, you signal to the speaker you are focused on them and

they matter. Listening is respect. Everyone needs to feel like

they have someone who will listen to them and listening

gives the speaker the opportunity to connect with you. While you are listening, you can collect data from which you can base further, deeper, meaningful conversations. Listening forges relationships.

Listening also fosters learning and promotes innovation and new ideas. Since the best leaders are always looking for ways to improve, listening promotes learning. I try to be slow to speak and quick to listen because I know the longer I listen, the more information I can gather and questions I might have about a particular topic are likely going to be answered. Listening also helps me generate questions for which, if not answered, I can gather what I need to know.

Listening will often spur me to new ideas. This is why I prefer to write my notes in longhand rather than type them (I am also a terrible typist). Taking notes, the old-fashioned way, allows for me to editorialize and scribble down ideas in the margin or use my highlighter for big ideas. I can personally brainstorm while listening. An added advantage to being a good listener is that your people will also share their great ideas with you. They know you are listening and that gives them the confidence to share.

Another part of listening is it promotes dialogue and discourse amongst your people. The best leaders are all team leaders at heart. They form teams and expect the leaders of those smaller teams to accomplish the missions assigned to them and take care of the people within their charge. Where speaking comes in is the best team leaders promote dialogue and discourse amongst their team members. It is critical to taking advantage of everyone's strengths and stimulating every team member to participating in the decision making process.

It is especially true to promote dialogue in group or public forums. It is never good to "squash" someone in front of their peers. For example, in a brainstorming session for new ideas, it is wrong to dismiss someone if you do not think

their idea will not work or does not keep with traditional

ideas. This is especially true in education where we have

doing things pretty much the same way since the industrial

revolution. Why would we not want unorthodox or "out of

the box" ideas? Besides, once someone is shut-down

publicly, they will naturally hesitate to make future

suggestions. This not only costs the team their input, but the

opportunity to see things from a different perspective

The point is, you never know when someone from

outside will have a good idea. Why would we want to do

anything to discourage their input? I am quite sure, many of

the best ideas and innovation came from this "out-of-the-

box" thinking. Why, in public education, where we complain

that things are so difficult to change, do we cling so tightly to

only traditional thought about what works? Also, what do

you think silencing people publicly does to morale and

loyalty? We have already suggested people in the intelligence building industry need to feel like they have a voice in operations. Shutting people down only turns them off and in an industry struggling to bring people in, the last thing we want to do is lose good people to other industries.

Written Communication

Excellent leaders express themselves well in writing. This does not mean you need to write a book or contribute to a weekly blog, but leaders' written products are clear, thoughtful, and articulate. Leaders produce works which are strong written documents free from grammatical or spelling errors and read easily. Leaders remember the audience. For example, if you are writing to parents, you need to avoid a lot of professional jargon, acronyms, and abbreviations. Your message needs to be as if you are writing to someone who knows absolutely nothing about what you are writing.

If you are writing to teachers, be sure to be respectful and very careful not to leave your messages open to hidden interpretation. Most writers know it is good practice to have someone proofread something before you send it out. In addition to proofreading my work, I ask a career teacher to read all of my teacher directed correspondence to ensure my message reads as I have intended. Nearly every time I prepare a correspondence for teachers I end up revising it based on input from colleagues and my products are always better after having been revised. I never want to sound critical or judgmental even when I am making a recommendation for improved practices. Remember tact is one of our leadership traits so we want our written correspondences as tactful as our spoken ones.

Typically, students will not be the most likely of your stakeholders to embrace your written products. Depending on their age, most students are more effectively addressed verbally though things like your morning announcements, or phone calls home. Sometimes though, school leaders need to prepare a written correspondence for students. If you decide you want to communicate with your students in writing than considering your audience is very important. Younger students will probably respond better to vivid colors and pictures with limited text. Older students can withstand more text, but stick with graphics and bullets for them too. Remember to try and get the information you want them to remember in short bursts emphasized with colors and other stresses.

The last thing I want to emphasize about written products is that you are 100% clear about what you are writing and you have considered what can be misinterpreted. Written products last forever and are subject to much more intense scrutiny and criticism than spoken words. You can always say "that is not what I meant" to something you said, but that is a lot more difficult when someone has something you have written. This is especially true with electronic communications like email and social media. It is always better to respond to a tricky situation in person, or at least over the phone, rather than replying in print or email. This is just another of those situations where you can either enhance or promote effective relationships or tear them down. We always want to take the opportunity to promote positive relationships and you have a much better shot at that using your spoken communication.

Non-verbal Communication

While there are conflicting schools of thought about which percentage of communication is non-verbal, suffice to say, quite a bit of what we communicate is through other than what we say. In fact, every one of us has probably been told, "it is not what you said, it is how you said it". Much of "how" we say things lies in the body language we communicated which accompanies what we say. Things like our body positioning, our facial expressions, and the way we use our hands all accompany, accent, and amplify our verbal communication making it very important we are aware of our body language.

I remember I had to give a pre-recorded speech once. I wrote an excellent speech, practiced in front of a mirror several times, and thought I was ready. The camera rolled and I delivered what I thought was an excellent speech (nailed it!). Checked it off my list and went on to my next mission. Later, the person who recorded the speech sent me a link for review and I was shocked at what I saw. While my words were clear, and my delivery fine, I rocked from side to side as if I was standing sideways on a see-saw through the entire speech. I was getting seasick watching it! Needless to say, I had to reconvene the video team and redo the speech.

My body language was awful and ruined an otherwise

excellent delivery.

Body language is another factor which can greatly

affect our relationships with people. Body language should

convey to the person with whom you are interacting they are

important and you have time for them. Things like standing

tall, making eye contact, smiling (when it is appropriate),

nodding approvingly, or tilting your head slightly to the side

all suggest you are fully engaged in the conversation. Other

gestures like crossing your arms, putting your hands on your

hips, or resting your head on your hands suggest you are

bored or even hostile. Other physical intimations like

twisting your hair, looking down, or rubbing your eyes, might

suggest you are distracted.

Improving your body language is difficult because

you do not always see yourself and what you are doing. Like

the aforementioned story, I had no idea I was rocking side to side, so I could not correct the movement on the spot (suffice to say I am aware of this tendency now though!). So, awareness of your own body language and how big of an impact it has on others is a great place to start. Watching yourself on video whenever possible can be a good step to seeing and reflecting on your own body language. Getting feedback from a coach or peer is also a great way to gather information on your own body language. Gathering the feedback from someone with whom you already have a trusting and strong relationship is best because you want honest feedback so you can make changes.

Another way to improve your body language is to mirror the person's mannerisms and gestures with whom you are interacting. Mirroring them sub-conscientiously tells them you approve of them and want to make a connection. Be careful not to over-do it or exaggerate the person's movements, so they do not feel like you are mimicking or making fun of them. Simply follow their lead and use the person's gestures like hand motions, facial expressions, and posture to guide your own. Studies have show this shows empathy and makes the person feel like to are relating to whatever they are telling you.

While it is difficult to determine exactly how much of our communication is non-verbal, we can assume enough to matter. With this in mind, it is important we are aware of our own body language and the impact it can have of our relationships and leadership effectiveness. Good leaders take the time to examine and reflect on their verbal and written communication, but how many of us take steps to improve our non-verbal communication? Improving our non-verbal communication is another way to improve as a leader and might be the difference we are looking for to become even more effective.

Communicating with Social Media

Most leaders today are finding there is no way to have a comprehensive communication plan without incorporating social media. This is not to say everyone needs to be digital leader of the year, or feel bad if they are not constantly posting, blogging, following, or liking. Without using social media though, you will find you are going to miss a large part of your stakeholders who use social media as their primary way of obtaining information. As a baby boomer, I take advantage of what social media has to offer while maintaining my generational distance.

Social media does have its advantages. First, many people use social media and are connected virtually 24/7. This is even more true with our students. If they are following you, they are very unlikely to miss a post. Next, many social media platforms can be set up to be one way. So, you can push out information and do not have to answer a lot of questions. And third, social media is a great way to build professional networks with other schools and organizations.

Social media does have its drawbacks though. There are some social media platforms I will not even look at because I know someone is saying something horrible or inappropriate about our school district. Therefore, it is important to avoid a few pitfalls. First, ensure to protect the privacy of the account. You would not want the password for the official school account falling into the wrong hands. Next, be careful who you follow. Nobody wants their school or district to be caught following something or someone controversial (or worse!) Finally, be sure to keep posts positive and always respect student and staff privacy. If your district has an opt out policy you want to be sure any announcements or recognition you put out does not violate any terms of privacy or student wishes.

The easiest way to manage the social media account is to assign it to the Chief Communications Officer or equivalent. If this is not possible or the responsibility falls on you, I recommend leaders set up a private account with the social media platform you want to learn first and start using it. Most of these "Apps" are pretty intuitive and tutorials exist if you need any assistance learning how to use them. Once you have the general idea how to follow, read, and send posts or updates, you can start with your organization's official social media account. I usually post two to three times a week with general reminders and re-post things from other organizations I trust. I keep things informative and light and never engage in two way conversations on social media.

Summing it up

There is just no substitute for effective communication and there is probably no other factor which effects a leader's relationship with the community they serve more than communication. For the purpose here, we addressed communication in three general forms. Mass communication means sending information to large groups of people like students, staff, parents and communities as a whole. Interpersonal communication means how we communicate individually with other people. There are four elements of interpersonal communication: listening, speaking, writing, and non-verbal. All forms of interpersonal communication impact our effectiveness as leaders and in our efforts to build relationships. To become a better communicator, it is important to first be self-aware. Other ways to enhance our communication is through rehearsal, having someone proofread our written communications, video recording ourselves, or using a coach, mentor, or peer to give us feedback. The third form of communication covered in this chapter was communicating through social media. Unfortunately, no communication plan can be the most effective today without including social media and leaders need to develop at least a nominal aptitude in communication through social media.

Putting this in to Practice

Reflection Question(s): How confident am I in my effectiveness of communicating with the stakeholders in my school or district?

Suggestions for Action: Pull out several examples of mass communication you have recently sent out to your stakeholders. Evaluate them for clarity, brevity, tone, and precision. If you have the opportunity, ask a colleague to review one or more pieces of your communication and offer feedback. Another idea is to find an example of one of your mass communications from several years ago and assess how or if your communications abilities, style, or methods have changed.

CHAPTER 6

Physical and Mental Wellness

I do not want to suggest nor even imply that great

leaders need to be ready to compete in the *American Ninja*

Warrior competition or the *World's Toughest Race*, but all

leaders should be physically fit and mentally well to lead

effectively at the highest level. This means taking care of your

body and mental health just as much as your intellect and

leadership skills. Leaders who are physically fit and healthy

are able to be at work more and withstand the rigorous pace

demanded by our jobs while we are engaged. Probably even

more importantly, even small improvements in any person's

health tangibly improves the quality of their life and the way

they feel every day. Who does not want to physically feel

better each day?

I spoke earlier in this text about the demands on

school administrators. It is not an exaggeration to suggest

many days for school leaders start as early as 6 AM and are not over until after 10 PM. Likewise, it is not unusual for school leaders to work six days a week. This is not written to scare anyone from becoming a school leader, but to illustrate that to maintain this kind of pace, leaders need to be physically fit and healthy. Otherwise, it is just a matter of time before they break down and cannot keep up with the rigors of their office or worse, have to miss work due to illness or fatigue. The nature of working in education is that school leaders cannot miss precious school days due to illness. There are just too few of them.

Also, as written in earlier sections, leaders need to set a good example. It is human nature to look up to people who are perceived as having discipline and self-control. Being healthy directly helps us become better at our jobs (no matter what they are), miss less time from work, and improves our quality of life. Good health and fitness habits transform our outlook, give us confidence, and can increase

our zest for life. Plus, from a very aesthetic perspective,

exercising and eating right can improve the way we look and

no matter how you feel about this, looks matter to a lot of

people who are watching their leaders.

Primer on Health

Improving health and fitness does not require a total

transformation of your lifestyle, but it does require changing

some habits permanently. Done effectively, shifting to a

healthier lifestyle can be done, and will transform you

though in many positive ways other than just the way you

look and feel. Change is hard for many people because the

habits they have developed in what they eat and drink, and

their levels of physical activity have taken sometimes

decades or longer of practice. This is a standard "good news-

bad news" scenario. The good news is everyone can change.

The bad news is it is not as easy as every infomercial and

product at GNC suggests.   This book is not about health and fitness, but being healthy and physically fit are directly linked to a leader's effectiveness.

Although many people without the requisite qualifications give health and/or fitness advice freely, I feel it would be irresponsible to do so if I were not qualified in this field. My time in the Marines allowed me to develop not only a strong commitment to health and fitness, but also academic, theoretical, and practical skills in creating, developing, and implementing health and fitness programs for individuals, small groups, and large groups. Following my career in the Marines, I worked as a Fitness Director with the YMCA and the Navy. I was a Certified Personal Trainer and taught group exercise in things like Boot Camp (imagine that!), cycling, running, and spinning. I am also a Master Fitness Specialist trained by the Cooper institute in Dallas

Texas. What follows is sound advice based on science, training, and personal experience.

My Friend Rob

I have a great friend Rob who is a fantastic school leader and an even better friend, parent, and father. A former coach, Rob transfers the best qualities of coaching into his job and gets great results. Of all the people I have worked with in education, Rob may be the best at establishing genuine, effective relationships with stakeholders regardless of their race, religion, sexual-orientation, or other difference. The reason why is because Rob definitely cares about all people and they know it. He can make a connection with virtually anyone and get results from there. He is super funny and fun to work with. The bond we had as co-workers was amazing and I love the guy both personally and professionally.

Unfortunately, Rob is not a particularly healthy guy. He will admit he has put on more than a few pounds as he has aged, his diet is terrible, and he rarely does any formal exercise. He is active with his family, and coaches his children's sports teams, and this with his demanding job, at least keeps him moving. Yet the rigors of his life put him under a lot of stress and pressure squeezing out time Rob should be investing in his own physical and mental health. I worry Rob is a "health timebomb" ready to go off at any minute.

A clear indicator of Rob's health is his work attendance. While he hates to miss work, and never does so without good reason, Rob tends to get sick- more than he should. In fact, it is not uncommon for Rob to miss days or even weeks during the school year due to a severe cold, the flu, or worse. Rob's lifestyle has him giving all he's got to everyone and everything around him until he can give no more and his body subsequently fails him. The result is that Rob then has to take time off from his job and his family to recuperate. I bet everyone has a friend like Rob and if you are like me, you worry about his health.

Diet and Health

If this is a sore subject, feel free to skip it, but if you struggle with your weight or feel like your diet is dragging you down, stick with me. Everyone needs their own motive for improving their health and fitness, but if becoming better at being a leader is not enough, find one. Your life literally depends on it! Once you have found your reason, here are a few ideas to help. While getting fit and healthy is not easy, you can start by simplify things and make great progress on improving your health by focusing on just four things.

First, decrease the amount of sugars you eat. Notice, I wrote "decrease". Don't try to eliminate sugars, just look to decrease them by like 20%. This is not as hard as it sounds because sugar is in virtually everything. Start reading labels

and know where you are taking in a lot of sugars and try to

switch up a few items to reduce the amount. Sugars in foods

are often cloaked as "carbohydrates". If you read a label and

a food is high in carbohydrates, it probably contains a lot of

sugar. There are also a lot of sugars in things like salad

dressing, catsup, and other condiments, and even certain

breads and cereals. Many of these products can even be

disguised as "healthy". Of course, all forms of alcohol

contain loads of sugar so if you want a sure fire way of

reducing calories and sugars, reduce or eliminate alcohol

from your diet. Start by cutting down on the sugar. Once you

get used to doing this, you can continue to make more

changes and they will not be as difficult.

The second easy thing to do is reduce the portion

sizes at every meal just a bit. I believe this is the biggest area

people go wrong when trying to "eat healthy". While it is

definitely good to eat what we know are healthy foods, if we eat too much of anything, we will gain weight no matter how "healthy" our choices. I have a friend who struggles with her weight despite eating numerous meals throughout the week which consist mainly of salad. The problem is her salads are enormous, and often contain things like processed meat, raisins, nuts, and dressings. These items are pure sources of sugar! Cut down on your portion sizes and your sugars and you greatly reduce your calories coming in.

Number three is to moderately increase your physical activity and make it regular. Before you do this however, you must be sure you are healthy enough to start working out. If you have any pre-existing health conditions, are over 40, or have just been sedentary for a length of time, please speak with your doctor before starting any type of new exercise. There is nothing wrong with seeing your doctor once in a while and definitely before making a lifestyle change like becoming more active. The final warning is to make sure you start in moderation. There is more on this to follow.

With the aforementioned demands of being a school administrator, you are probably thinking, "Where do I find the time to exercise"? In fact, the mention of exercise might have caused you to tune me out, but please try to tune back in and stick with me. One of the many great things about physical activity is it serves as what I like to call a "force multiplier". A force multiplier is a term used in military science which means a resource or factor which increases a person or groups effectiveness without increasing its effort. So, making time for exercise will actually make you more productive during the times you are not exercising thus creating the time you need to exercise.

Why does exercise serve as a "force Multiplier"? There are many reasons. First, as I wrote, the human being is the greatest organism ever created. One of our fantastic and

unexplained abilities of our bodies is it heals better and

stronger after certain tissues have been damaged or put

under stress. This is especially true with muscles. When we

exercise, we actually cause damage to our muscles which,

when healed in just a couple of days, heal stronger and

bigger than before they were injured. Bigger and stronger

muscles allow for us to move more things faster. It can

increase our pace of virtually doing everything, thus

increasing our productivity.

Exercise also improves the efficiency in which our

body works. Our resting heart rate slows, our respiratory

efficiency improves, and our digestive and other bodily

functions advance. When our body functions better, we think

more clearly, complete tasks more efficiently, we sleep

better, and our outlook improves based on both the

combination all of the above factors and the synergy created by them all happening at once. So, the fact is, you do have

time to exercise because once you start exercising, the effect

of activity creates even more time. You become

disproportionally more efficient with the time you have

remaining when compared to the time you lost exercising.

Modest changes to Diet and Physical Activity

This math matters. If you cut sugars and calories by

10% and increase activity by 10% (both of which are very

doable goals), you have just created a calorie deficit of

approximately 20%. Think about this, if you have been

coasting along in life taking in 4000 calories a day (28,000 per

week- which is way too many by the way), cutting intake by

10% and increasing expenditure by 10% creates a potential

calorie deficit of 600-800 calories per day or between 4200

and 5600 calories a week! With each pound of body mass

worth about 3500 calories, you have potentially just lost up

to 1.5 pounds. That could be 15 pounds in ten weeks.

This leads me to my fourth and final suggestion which is to commit yourself to the inputs and the outputs will take care of themselves. Change is easy, transformation is hard. To transform yourself, you should start slow and make changes which can more easily be maintained. For example, it is much easier to find one thing in your diet which is high in sugar and eliminate it rather than trying to restrict yourself from everything you have been eating for years. Slow and steady wins the race. I will explain in the next section some very common reasons people start health and fitness initiatives and fail.

Why We Struggle

In my experience as a personal trainer there were several very common scenarios which aggravated people's efforts to make healthy initiatives permanent. In the first example of why people might struggle to stick with a health and fitness initiative, a person wants to improve their health and fitness or lose weight so much, their efforts while well intended, are too aggressive. They make dramatic changes to their lives like joining a gym or trying one of the many proprietary weight loss products. They make amazing progress in the first month. They look great. They feel great. Their production soars and their sleep is amazing. Their blood pressure falls to normal range and they feel energized all the time. They have never looked or felt better and people are even commenting on how great they look.

The problem is that after about a month, reality kicks in. You see, another amazing thing about the human body is it will fight against starvation and becomes skeptical to taking on the change. The immediate response from the body when confronted with aggressive calorie deprivation is to protect itself. The body clings to its energy sources because it knows it needs the energy for life sustaining activities like respiration, metabolism, and digestion. Naturally, weight loss becomes more difficult despite the same level of effort. For the once motivated and progressing dieter, progress slows and they become discouraged.

Unfortunately, following an aggressive attempt at weight loss and fitness, there is a second response from both the dieter and the dieter's body. The dieters become discouraged and return to their previous habits. As stated, the body responds and because they are in a phase of holding tight to calories, it holds on to the new increased intake by the once committed dieter even tighter. In many cases the now discouraged dieter has slowed or even stopped their exercise routine. They rapidly gain weight and give back any progress they had made. Sometimes they gain even more weight from where they started. This is the story of the yoyo dieter.

In scenario two, someone makes a commitment to health and fitness and again aggressively starts to exercise and watch what they eat. They jump on the scale after the first week (usually around January 7th), and do not see any weight loss. The person in this scenario might be discouraged but thinks they could have tried a bit harder and decides to really commit themselves in week two. January 14th comes around and they again get on the scale. Nothing. No weight loss and maybe even weight gain! The person in this scenario becomes discouraged and either immediately or eventually just gives up and returns to their unhealthy habits.

The reasons for the lack of success for this person are often the same as the person in the first scenario. Their bodies have responded to the aggressive attempts to shed mass by protecting itself and holding on to their source of energy. In another scenario, the person might have selected the wrong type of exercise program, or actually increased their intake (because exercise can make you hungry!), and might be getting stronger but not losing weight. Since we know muscle weighs more than fat, the person does not see weight loss so assumes their program is not working. Similar to the person in scenario one, they become discouraged and give up. This is why small adjustments made over longer periods of time make a difference.

In yet another example of someone attempting to improve their health and fitness habits and failing, the person gets injured. Their enthusiasm to get back into shape quickly has them starting too fast and they break down. After a long lay-off from exercise, it is crucial to build your body's tolerance to exercise slowly so your joints, bones, and ligaments can withstand an increased load without suffering too much trauma. This is yet another reason to take things slow and focus on small changes which you can make permanent. There is no reason to start on an aggressive exercise program, get injured, and then not be able to exercise at all.

Finally, another big reasons people fail to stick with a health and fitness initiative is that we have been conditioned to getting what we want immediately and with little effort. Want to know the 24th President of the United States? It takes about four seconds to find out. How about the distance between Denver and Seattle? Three seconds. Need a recipe for smoked salmon? In about this same amount of time (three or four seconds) you can have unlimited recipes in the palm of your hand. Improving your health and fitness levels take time and effort, but human beings have become more and more accustomed to getting what they want almost immediately. They are not inclined to wait for anything. Often times, people who start eating better and exercising and do not see immediate results give up because they are not used to having to wait.

A Few Words on the "Best" Exercise

Trainers are often asked, "what is the best type of exercise"? The correct answer is, the best exercise to do is the one you are willing to do regularly. I will say, perhaps against some schools of exercise science, and with the risk of making a lot of readers cringe, no exercise is better for cardio vascular conditioning and weight loss than running- outside, on the road or trail. This is not to say I recommend you go out and start an aggressive running program. Running is not for everyone, and there is a lot of risks associated with running, especially for older adults and those with pre-existing health factors. If you think running is for you, do some research and start very slowly.

I say this because, there truly are certain exercises which will work better than others depending on a person's fitness goals, experiences, habits, and likes. Nonetheless, far and away the best exercise for you is the one you will commit to and participate in regularly. A type of exercise like running, which has proven to be effective, is of no use to you if you cannot or will not do it. For some people running may be appropriate. For others walking, biking, swimming, aerobics classes, kickboxing, or one of the many aerobic machines at the gym might be the choice for you (but you do not *have* to go to the gym)! There are even a lot of exercises you can do right from the privacy of your own home. Technology has made free fitness classes available to us in the palms of our hands.

Whatever exercise you choose to do, it should be aerobic (with oxygen, meaning you can sustain the exercise for longer periods of time without getting completely out of breath), and you need to do it regularly. Take it slow and increase your volume and pace of exercise with proficiency. It is normal to feel some stiffness or soreness after starting a new exercise program, but if you feel any pain, or the soreness keeps you from exercising again, you'll know you went too hard. Like I wrote earlier in this chapter, just be sure to start in moderation and stick with it.

Sports can also serve to get you active. Many of us play golf or tennis, pick-up basketball, or other sports which are great to get us active and often stimulate social relationships which we need to strengthen our mental health. If something like this has been a part of your lifestyle and you are still struggling with your health and fitness, then obviously it is not enough and you need to either add some aerobic activities to your plan or shift from sports and games to aerobic exercise. If sports are something you once did and could do again, try it. Whatever exercise you are willing to make as a regular part of your lifestyle is the best one.

There are many ways we can also increase our calorie expenditure without formal exercise. When I was a building principal, I made it a point to walk every hall and stairwell in the school following every hall change I could. I brought in a "stand-up" desk and spent as much time on my feet as I could. When choosing recreational activities for my family, my wife and I always leaned towards activities which required us to walk or do some other form of physical activity like biking or swimming. When going to the grocery store, try to park as far away from the door as possible. Walk or bike whenever you can and make very explicit choices to be active. There are many others if you just have the mindset that you will incorporate movement into everything you can throughout your normal routine.

Should I get a Trainer?

Most people just starting to get back into shape do not need to invest in a trainer, join a gym, or buy expensive products. If you have a pair of "go fasters" (the Marine word for gym shoes), and seasonal clothing, you can start your program today for virtually nothing. I understand though, some people insist that they just cannot get motivated to do it on their own. They need the commitment shelling out a few bucks to force them to exercise and eat better. If you fall into this category, I ask you to reconsider because as Pink wrote in his amazing book "Drive", intrinsic motivation will trump extrinsic motivation every time (Pink, 2009). Recognizing you need to get fit and healthy because it is the best thing for you, rather than to extract value from your investment is much more likely to make your desire to change reach long-term fruition.

If you need the extra motivation however, I suggest you invest in a friend before you invest in any trainer, diet product, or exercise equipment. Seek a colleague or associate interested in making the journey with you and work-out together. Better yet, find a small group of friends willing to make the commitment. Maybe you can even ask your spouse or significant other to join you! The same way exercise can enhance your work life, it can enhance your personal life. It can lead to making new friends, improving relationships through a common struggle, and strengthening bonds with people with the shared interest of self-improvement. If getting a trainer or joining a gym is the only way you are willing to start being healthier, then go for it, but finding friends or loved ones to join you is typically more effective and definitely more rewarding.

Mental Health

Our jobs take up on average eight hours of our waking day- often more. This is about one-third of our adult lives. We rely on our jobs for income, for personal and professional satisfaction, and in even our identity. Our jobs are stressful. People depend on us and we are responsible for them. Because of this, our jobs have a tremendous impact on our mental and emotional well-being.

Many of the principles and strategies in this book are going to help you with your mental health. Becoming better at your job for example, cuts down on stress and the unknown things which can bog down many people making them anxious or upset. Focusing on relationships reduces stressful conversations, conflict, and confrontations. Effective communication contributes to workplace harmony as everyone feels informed and valued, and of course, being physically fit and healthy causes you to mentally feel better about yourself, reduces worry, and makes you more productive. Finally living your life with faith gives you the confidence that you will defeat every challenge and keeps things in the right perspective. Using these tools to become a better leader not only increases your productivity, it improves your outlook, your demeanor, and your quality of life.

I believe another key to good mental health is achieving balance. It stands to reason that if we are consumed by our work, then our mental health will be tied directly to whatever is going on there. If things are going well and life at work is good, we feel good. If there is a crisis however, we become the crisis. This is worse when we treat everything as a crisis! When we are out of balance, we become our work instead of the other way around. We all need outlets outside of work which give us joy. Our families, our activities, and our interests need to be present in our lives to allow us to experience pleasures which are not available in the workplace.

Finally, if the practices and principles in this book do not help you with your mental health and you find yourself not enjoying what you are doing, please seek professional help. Most jobs have resources for their employees and you cannot be afraid to take advantage of things like counseling or group therapy. Life is hard, but fortunately, there are people who can help when it becomes too difficult to go at it alone.

Summing it up

Effective leaders must be physically and mentally fit to withstand the rigorous demands of leadership. This starts with health and fitness. While no leader needs to be ready to go out and compete in the *"Iron Man World Championships"*, every leader needs to be healthy and active. Health and fitness practices not only make us feel better about ourselves, we look better, gain confidence, and earn respect from our peers who recognize our commitment and personal discipline. Being healthy and fit also allows us to make better use of the time we spend working. We are more efficient, more effective, and can actually get more done with the time we have when we are fit.

To start on getting fit and healthy, go slow and make small changes which can more easily be made permanent. There are four things you can do to start becoming healthier today. First reduce your sugar intake. Next, reduce meal portion sizes. Then moderately increase your level of physical activity, and finally, take it slow to make becoming healthier a long term lifestyle change.

The last thing all leaders need to do is take care of their own mental health. Start with the principles and practices in this book to amplify your skills as a leader increasing your productivity and enhancing your work relationships. Then seek balance in your life by spending time with family, friends, and engaging in enjoyable activities or hobbies. Finally, if this does not help, take advantage of outside resources. Many people need the support of a counselor, therapist, or group to help them find peace, comfort, and security. People need you to be your best self and if you are struggling internally, you cannot be that for them or more importantly for you.

Putting this into Practice

Reflection Question(s): How do you assess your current physical and mental health? How satisfied are you with your level of health and fitness and your ability to be your best self?

Suggestions for Action: Imagine yourself and your productivity both at work and at home if you were in optimal physical and mental health. Make a short bulleted list of things in your life which could improve if you became healthier and more fit.

CHAPTER 7

Having Faith

Jon Gordon has written a bunch of great books about leadership. In his book *The Power of Positive Teams* Jon tells us we have a choice. We can live our lives either with fear or with faith (Gordon, 2018). If we live our lives in fear, we are constantly reacting to things with the expectation the worst is inevitable. When we have faith, we know things will work out and we will prevail. It is kind of like the self-fulfilling prophesy. If we think the worst is going to happen, it probably will.

"Rudy" is one of my favorite movies. If you do not know the story, the main character is a small, average athlete who joins the Notre Dame Football team as a "walk-on" and actually plays in a game. A "walk-on" player is one who was not recruited or offered a scholarship. These players simply try out for the team and a few of the lucky ones are selected to be a part of the program. Rarely though do they dress for games and even more rarely are they given the chance to play. To play in a Division I athletic competition as a walk-on player is exceptional- especially in football. "Rudy" is a great underdog story.

One character in the movie is a priest. In a scene where he is counselling Rudy who is begging for a chance to be a part of the Notre Dame program, the priest tells him "Son, there are two things I know. First, there is a God. Second, it is not me" (Anspaugh, 1993). I tell this story because I am a spiritual person and I agree wholeheartedly with the priest in "Rudy". I believe in God and know in my own heart, I am just a tiny, tiny part of His great plan. So, I put my faith fully in God, and I live my life knowing I can trust in God to watch over me and those I pray for. Further, I genuinely believe in God's will being done here on Earth. Leaving things up to God does not relieve me of any responsibilities, but it does take a lot of weight off of my shoulders when I can trust Him with all things. I have faith and let God do the heavy lifting.

However, I know everyone is not spiritual and does not believe in God or a higher power. If you are someone who does not put your faith in God, you can still be faithful in other ways. For you, having faith can mean believing in your own preparation and abilities to make good decisions and employ resources effectively to accomplish your mission. It can mean knowing you have a professional staff who will make good choices and accomplish their mission. Faith for you might even mean knowing things have worked out for hundreds of years before us and will work out again no matter the reason.

Faith can also mean believing you have the kind of team which will respond effectively to every crisis. Your team and the way you have prepared them is another good reason to have faith. A well trained team is proactive and lets you

know what is going on. You all communicate together, laugh

together, and cry together. I used to work with a guy who

would say "keep the principal informed. You don't want her

hit in the face with a fish when she walks in in the morning".

It is great to have the faith that your team will never let you

get "hit in the face with a fish".

Faith can also give us confidence and resolve to stay

the course and do what we believe is best for children 100%

of the time. Let me give you an example. As a school leader I

have always held a strong belief that nearly all students can

achieve at the highest levels but have been separated over

the years into High, Medium, and Low achieving categories.

In most schools or districts, you are likely to see "Honors" or

"Advanced" programs where classes are more rigorous or

"faster". The highest achieving (aka: best behaved) students

usually end up in these classes. Then there will be the

"standard" or "academic" courses where, you know, the "regular" students go. Things in those classes certainly meet the standards, they just get to them at a *slower* pace. Finally, some systems will even have "basic" or "remedial" courses where students who are behind are given "extra" help to get them caught up (Hint: Most never do).

As I stated, I believe, A) humans are all organically intelligent, and B) nearly all can learn at the highest levels. I also believe, if someone is deficient at something, giving them less of it will not make them more proficient. What I mean is if someone is a weight-lifter and wants to get stronger, the solution is probably not to go to the gym and lift less weight. The solution would be to lift more weight, and associate with other people with weightlifting skills who are also interested in getting stronger. Similarly, if you wanted to learn all you could possibly learn about birds, you would need an intense bird learning program. You would need the most detailed and well instructed program about birds you could find. You would not want a modestly intense bird learning program or a slower bird learning program. You would want birds, birds, and nothing but birds.

Unfortunately, what we often do in schools is to take all of our students we have judged as less proficient and put them together in the same "standard" or "basic" programs. Then we narrow the curriculum (or worse) often depriving them of grade level information. Oh yeah! We typically assign our least experienced or less proficient teachers to these classes. Now, not only do the students lose out on the benefit of the most rigorous and highest quality instruction, and often the best or most experienced teachers, we remove all of the best peer models for them to emulate. We deliberately give them less when they need more. It is counterintuitive.

So, my second year into my first principalship, our team decided we would begin "de-tracking" our classes with the intent of having all Honors classes and above within three years (have I mentioned my belief in the power of heterogeneous grouping?). This went over mostly as you would imagine, with certain factions of the school and community pushing back for some legitimate, but mostly unfounded reasons. Surprisingly though, once we weathered the initial storm and push-back, we were able to stay on course and were de-tracking courses systematically by content and grade level at a rate of several per year and things worked out splendidly. Our overall results in the classes improved and results in the groups of students who were moved up from standard to Honors level classes improved dramatically. Moreover, discipline and school culture improved noticeably.

My purpose in telling this story is not to champion

for de-tracking (although I do!). The purpose is to illustrate

how our leadership team had to maintain faith through this

process to make it work. De-tracking classes at our school

was a tremendous risk and it would have been easy to

whither and give up. Test scores were already high and we

had hundreds of students in Advanced Placement courses.

Our traditional students were doing well and enjoying their

isolation from what they thought were less serious students

(or worse). Many in our staff and our community did not

want anything to do with this either. Teachers had it in their

minds that grouping students into advanced, medium, and

slow categories was the best and only way to teach and we

were going to shortchange one or even all of the groups of

students while mixing them together. Worse, we were asking

them to change the way they taught. They were going to

really have to differentiate!

As we stuck with it though we collected more and more advocates for giving every student in the school the opportunity to learn at the highest levels. By the time I left the school we had increased participation in Advanced Placement courses by all students and increased the rate of participation at even higher rates with students from traditionally underrepresented groups. Additionally, nearly every student in the school was enrolled in at least one Honors level course or higher. When I say nearly every student, I am talking over 99%. We were also able to tow the line on outcomes. Despite nearly every student in the school stepping up in rigor, both grades and test scores improved. Our team kept the faith and faith pulled us through.

Summing it up

Faith is what we have when we believe in someone or something we do not always see. Jon Gordon writes that we can live our lives with faith or with fear (Gordon, 2018).

Living in fear often means we are looking for the worst to happen to. When we live with faith, we trust in something to carry us through and everything is going to be OK. Personally, I am a spiritual person and believe in God. I pray often for wisdom and believe to my core if God's will is done on earth, everything will be OK. For me, I put my faith in God above all other things.

Everyone does not believe in God or a higher power but still needs faith. The alternative is to live in fear. Faith for some might be faith in their training or preparation, or faith in the system they have built. Faith to others might lie in believing their friends or family will be there for them no matter what. For others, they might have faith in tools or resources they use to do their jobs. No matter what you choose, you must have faith to be able to motivate, inspire, and influence others.

We need to have faith because we have literally no idea what tomorrow brings. If we walk around fearful that the worst is going to happen, it probably will. Conversely, if we live our lives knowing we have been prepared for the worst whatever it is, we know things will work out and we will succeed. Having faith simply means having confidence we are prepared. In my case, I am prepared by my faith in my Lord and Savior. For others they are prepared by their skills, training, and preparation. The best leaders have faith.

Putting this into Practice

Reflection Question(s): What degree do you live your life with faith rather than worry? What are the areas in your life where you let worry or fear drive your decision making or behavior?

Suggestions for Action: Make a list of things of which you have a good reason to be fearful leaving space under each item. Then below each item for which you are fearful,

counter the fear with something in which you can have faith.

Example:

Fear/Worry- I worry that I will follow in the footsteps of my

Dad and have the same sort of health problems which

plagued him.

Faith- I lead a healthy lifestyle, see my doctor regularly, and

eat right. Medicine is advancing every day to help people

with all sorts of medical problems. Having the same health

problems as my Dad is not a foregone conclusion.

CHAPTER 8

Improving your Leadership Skills

There are tons of great ways to improve your leadership skills, and every leader should make becoming a better leader a part of their mission. If you remember, one of the Marine Corps leadership principles is "know yourself and seek self-improvement", and one of the *Leading Made Simple* principles is "always reflect on your own practices and seek ways to continuously improve". Both of these principles suggest a commitment to continuously taking stock of your abilities and effectiveness and finding ways to increase effectiveness and productivity to be a better leader.

Learning started off for me pretty much like everyone else. It was something I had to do. As I grew though and started to see the benefits from learning and professional growth, being a lifelong learner has become a way of life. Probably because I know I have many shortcomings, I enjoy being reflective, and working on myself

every chance I get. Mainly, I love learning because as an

educator, I love education. We all should. I am a life-long

learner by choice and whether I am reflecting on an

exchange I had with a stakeholder, reviewing a district-wide

correspondence I sent out, or learning sixth grade math again

with my daughter, I absolutely love the process of learning.

I also feel learning and improving is a professional

obligation. Something that is personally frustrating to me as

an educational leader is seeing other educators not taking

personal growth seriously. With respect to relationships,

(which I see as '*1a*' to professional competence), professional

competence is more than likely the most important factor

which influences our effectiveness as a teacher and teacher

leader. We can have the best relationships in the world but if

our skills and content knowledge are poor, relationships will

not help us. Because of this we need to constantly reflect,

learn, and improve our professional competence. This can only be achieved with a commitment to professional growth.

Another reason to work on our leadership skills is to set a good personal example. This advice also stems directly from the Marine Corps leadership principles ("set the example") and *Leading Made Simple* principles ("set the example and model the behaviors and practices you wish to see"). We know and teach modeling as a method of stimulating the behaviors and practices we want to see, so as educational leaders we need to model lifelong learning and a show everyone we have a growth mindset.

There are formal and informal ways to improve our leadership skills. The formal learning opportunities include things like taking classes, attending conferences, or even presenting at conferences just to name a few. There are also many informal and impromptu way to improve. What follows, in no particular order, are some formal and informal ideas to hone your skills as a leader. While this list is certainly not all-inclusive, it gives leaders some ideas to implement into their routines on their way to continuous improvement.

The first and perhaps easiest way to improve your leadership skills is to treat every circumstance as an opportunity to be a better leader. I was listening to audible book recently (I hesitate to share more information about the book because it was so terrible). At one point in the book the author read that "we have to always remember everything we do has an impact on those around us so we need to be very conscious of what we want that impact to be". Brilliant! The experience of spending countless hours listening to this awful book, a 99.9% lose-lose experience, allowed me to learn or be reminded of that one nugget of good information. This example shows leaders, by using every opportunity to grow, can constantly pursue self-improvement without having to rely solely on courses, conferences, or other formal learning opportunities.

Leaders must also be explicitly organized. Therefore, another thing every leader must do is develop a foolproof method of personal organization. Some people have a natural ability to remember everything. Most of us do not and we need to learn a system so that we do not forget things like dates, numbers, and deadlines. Fortunately, technology has evolved with so many good tools and resources, staying organized is becoming easier and easier. Some people still like pencils and paper, but whatever the system you decide upon, the trick is finding a method which is water-tight and ensures you are where you are supposed to be and do what you are supposed to do. Remember that one of the leadership traits is dependability and finding a foolproof method of organization increases your ability to be dependable.

Keep Good Company

Another method of personal leadership improvement is to find ways to spend time with other high quality leaders. This is best if the leaders you spend time with are in the type of job in which one day you might want to serve. The leaders I serve alongside in my current role are all of the highest quality. They have been in the field for decades, and have risen to the top of their profession. Yet, some of them stand out amongst the rest. What I notice about the leaders who really stand out among us is they are constantly seeking opportunities to lead and share outside our immediate group. They join various committees and boards and report back to us their findings and the work their committees are doing. By seeking opportunities to lead in areas even above their executive duties, they both improve their own skills and attain a position among the rest of us as leaders of leaders.

I experienced this personally after a good friend of mine asked me to replace him as our district representative on an executive board. He sold me on the idea by telling me "You'll just have to show up once a month and take notes and bring them back to share with the district". Boy was that wrong! I found that the members of the committee were some of the strongest and most vocal leaders in the state and I had to really do my homework to be prepared to interact with such a complex thinking group of leaders. The great thing is after two year on the Board, I was comfortable among those higher order thinkers and had grown immensely in both my own knowledge and experience. I found that seeking interactions with high level thinkers caused me to think and work at levels I never thought possible.

While the best leaders do it for the right reasons, often being an effective leader creates new opportunities for us personally. I think most people in their field want to move up and get promoted into higher positions, often in leadership. One of the best ways any leader can move up in his or her field is to watch his or her own supervisor and seek out the skills needed to do the supervisor's job. That might mean enrolling in certain course work, taking standardized leadership assessments, or gaining certain experiences like working with committees or leading teams of peers. Doing things like these not only get you ready, they signal to those doing the hiring that you have the skills that will later translate to being a good leader. Don't wait until you need a particular endorsement or qualification. Take care of it now so when your opportunity opens up, you meet the requisite qualifications.

Another thing aspiring leaders need to do is to maintain good company. My Dad used to have a phrase: "if you sleep with dogs, you get fleas" (what a horrible thought).

His point was, no matter my own character, the character of those with whom I kept the most company was going to rub off on me. Find the kind of people in your industry who are of the highest caliber and from whom you can learn with every interaction. Not only do you benefit from the tangible learning opportunities which come along with listening to and watching good leaders, you benefit from your association with someone who others look up to and respect.

Leaders are Readers

The best leaders read often. By reading, I mean print material other than social media! Reading stimulates our brain and trains us to focus and pay attention. Whether leaders are reading books or articles about their trade, or they are reading for entertainment, leaders should be readers. Reading hones and improves all of our communication skills and sharpens our vocabulary and grammar. Reading informs us and teaches us (know yourself and seek self-improvement). Reading improves our reading

skills so when we have to find information in print, our skills

are sharp and refined.

Keep teaching

The best leaders also teach other leaders. This should

be easy because the majority of educational leaders are

former classroom teachers. I learned very early in my life as a

professional the best way to learn something was to teach it

to someone else. Teaching something to someone else really

reinforces our knowledge of the subject causing us to know

the subject in depth. I was reminded of this as a young

sergeant in the Marine Corps going through Drill Instructor

School in 1991.

DI School, as we called it, was and probably still is,

one of the most rigorous, demanding schools in the Marines.

For starters, only the most physically fit and highly motivated

Marine non-commissioned officers get selected to attend the

school. The attrition rate is extremely high. In my class at DI

school, about 33 men started the 12 week course and 19 of

us finished (only men attended the course in San Diego- men

and women attend the DI School in Parris Island, South

Carolina). The physical and mental demands of the course

are designed to train Marines to make Marines. Frankly,

falling short of the rigorous standards is nothing of which to

be ashamed. DI School is just that difficult.

Aside from the physical demands of the course which

are continuous and extremely arduous, the mental demands

are uncommonly rigorous. One example of this is the

learning of the Marine Corps Drill and Ceremonies Manual

(Drill Manual) through a process called "teach backs". The

Marine Corps Drill and Ceremonies Manual is a voluminous

book of literally hundreds of different drill movements and

was required to be memorized verbatim by the students. To

put this in perspective, imagine having to memorize a book

word for word about the size of a standard encyclopedia

volume, full of information written in a language you are just

learning.

For testing, the Marine being assessed would

position himself at one end of a large open space called the

parade deck with the evaluator standing across from him

about 75 yards away. The testing Marine was required to

shout the instruction (teach it back- again verbatim) across

the parade deck to the evaluating instructor who was taking

points off for any words out of order, any missing words

(Including small ones like "of" and "the"), incorrect

pronunciations, or anything else which sounded out of sort.

This process was followed for every movement in the manual

and took place over the entire 12 weeks with Marines being

assessed in this area every few days.

To graduate from DI School and become a drill instructor is a great honor in itself. Every class though has one Marine who distinguishes himself above all other Marines in the class and is awarded a sword which is the symbol of the Marine Non-Commissioned Officer (NCO). Yet, while it is the goal of every Marine starting DI School to be the course honor graduate and receive the NCO Sword, most decide fairly quickly they just want to survive and graduate. Finishing as number one in the class usually winds up coming down to just a few very ready Marines.

At the end of each week of DI School, students meet with their "squad advisor" for a conference. At this conference, the student receives a report of where they generally stand in the class. After about week three every student is given their actual numerical standing in the class. I was shocked to find after week three of DI School I sat I the top five of all of my classmates.

About that time, I made the decision I was going be the course honor graduate, and I confined myself to nothing but studying and training. I became absolutely obsessed with reading, memorizing, studying, and working out physically. I carried index cards in my pocket and studied them at every opportunity. I studied during breakfast, lunch, and dinner and was sure I was going to move up when I got my next evaluation. But several weeks went by and each week I would find I had only moved up slightly in the standings. I had no idea what I could do more, so I just resolved to myself that I would continue to do my best and be satisfied with the outcome either way.

A strange thing happens when people are under stressful conditions. In the case of the students in my DI School class in 1991, like I am sure happened in many others, the students eventually banded together under the strain of the course and the immense pressure of the instructors who, incidentally are all top accomplished drill instructors. As students in the class began dropping all around us, those of who remained, naturally banded together in an effort to make it through.

The students formed study teams, worked together, shouted teach backs to each other, ran together, did pull-ups together, and augmented each other's weaknesses. Ultimately, I found when I helped others, my own skills improved even more than when I was spending every minute of the waking day grinding away alone. Each week I saw myself moving up in the rankings until around week nine I sat at number one in the class with three weeks to go.

The last three weeks crawled by as we completed our final assessments, inspections, physical fitness tests, and teach-backs, all which counted, and all which increased in both difficulty and weight towards our final standing. In the end, I was awarded the NCO Sword as the Honor Graduate of

DI School Class 3-91, San Diego California. I know now I never could have done it without learning that helping others learn helped me learn even better. Later, I applied this strategy as a student at the Marine Corps Staff Non-Commissioned Officer's Leadership Training Academy and then again during the Marine Corps Advanced Staff Non-Commissioned Officer's Leadership Training Academy. I was the Honor graduate at both those courses as well.

Find a Coach, Be a Coach

Another topic closely related to leadership of which many books, articles, and blogs have been written is coaching. Every one of us can benefit from having a coach. The way I look at it, if legendary golfer Tiger Woods and multiple time Olympic gold medalist Michael Phelps can benefit from coaching, so can everyone else. The best leaders, and the best organizations for that matter, lead from a coaching perspective. To get you motivated about coaching, I recommend you watch Atul Guwande's 2017 Ted

Talk where he talks about how coaching helped him as a top

surgeon (Guwande, 2017).

For the purpose of this book, the coach to whom I

am referring does not wear a ball cap or blow a whistle. He

or she is not standing with hands on knees watching you and

shouting plays or orders as you work. Coaching, for this

purpose and from my own, untrained perspective, is simply a

relationship formed between at least two people with the

intent on improving performance. Coaches interact with us

at a professional level and serve as another option for self-

improvement.

All good professional leaders should serve as

coaches, and all good leaders should seek coaching

relationships for themselves. Coaches provide us with

someone to objectively review our performance and assist us

in arriving at methods or strategies we can employ to help us get better. Since the best leaders are always trying to be more effective, coaching is a great vehicle for this. Coaching others helps us become better leaders just like teaching improves our knowledge and expertise on the topics we teach.

Coaching works at every level and there does not need to be a hierarchy established between the coach and the person being coached. In fact, I believe in the professional context, coaching actually works better when there is no sort of senior-subordinate relationship. The coach can better serve to provide objective insight and feedback and the person being coached open to assessing the feedback when there is no threat or risk of evaluation.

There is a real science to coaching which I do not have the pages to discuss here, but the coaching relationship differs from other relationships. It can be informal and friendly, or impersonal and direct. The term "coaching" though suggests a more parallel relationship where the coach

feels comfortable to give feedback and the coached is open

to evaluating the feedback and putting it into practice.

Coaching also relies on the coaches' ability to gauge what the

needs are of the person being coached. Does he or she need

to be taught something or just asked questions until he or

she comes up with the answer? One of the many benefits

coaching provides is the flexibility for the coach to respond to

the relationship the most effective way.

Summing it up

Elements of both the Marine Corp Leadership

principles and the *Leading Made Simple* leadership principles

suggest the best leaders continuously seek to improve their

abilities and skills. There are many ways leaders can seek

self-improvement. Of course, leaders should take advantage

of every formal opportunity to learn and lead, but there are

also many informal opportunities. Formal training

opportunities include things like taking classes and attending seminars or conferences.

Informal learning opportunities are numerous. For starters every leader should be using every experience as an opportunity to learn and grow. Next, leaders should seek out mentors and maintain the company of people who can influence their skills. The best leaders are always looking to move up in responsibility so they watch senior leaders and supervisors so then the time comes to step in and do the jobs of the higher leaders they are ready.

Leaders are readers. They need to read both for technical knowledge and for entertainment. Reading not only teaches us, it improves our written and verbal communication skills like diction and vocabulary. We learn from reading and keep our skills sharp in case we have to read for understanding. Leaders read and readers lead.

Leaders seek out opportunities to share and teach with their colleagues and subordinate leaders. They never forget they are teachers and teacher leaders so they hone their craft by presenting as often as possible. Leaders should seek a coach and be a coach. A coach can objectively let us know how we can improve or help us arrive at this information through a series of deliberate questions. Serving as a coach for someone else keeps our skills sharp and increases our opportunities for dialogue with other leaders.

Putting this into Practice

Reflection Question(s): How am I using every event in my life as an opportunity to learn and grow as a leader?

Suggestions for Action: Make a list of as many learning events in your recent memory and what you learned. Then, reflect on how the event will affect future leadership actions in the future. If you can, get your team together and try this activity with them. Once everyone has their list, share it with

each other and have a discussion.

CHAPTER 9

What's Next?

Whether you are an experienced leader or just starting out, one of the many tenets of great leadership is to assimilate quickly and then, as discussed in chapter eight, constantly improve. So, what's next? How do you take the words from the preceding pages and be the leader everyone wants to work with and be around? How do you improve so you can lead your team to accomplishing your mission and maybe even prepare yourself for higher levels of leadership and responsibility? What follows are some starting points. Many of these things you may already do- especially if you are already very effective. Other things might give you an idea how to tweak you own approach to improve even more.

For starters, we need to go back to the beginning and remember the only two real ways to measure the effectiveness of a leader are by mission accomplishment and troop welfare. If you are doing those two things 100% of the time, then you are a great leader. As discussed in chapter eight, this does not mean your job is done and you can put your cue in the rack. In education, we are in a continuous state of improvement, so one of your many implied missions as an educator is to continuously improve so you can better serve your students and your community. Therefore, the first thing you can do to put *Leading Made Simple* into practice is to commit yourself to being in a continuous state of growth. Just like the Marine's first principle of leadership reads, "know yourself and seek self-improvement".

Leadership is a Contact Sport

It is extremely important to know that leadership is a contact sport. Great leaders do not lead from a distance and they cannot expect to get results parked in meetings all day or holed up in their office. This is common advice from most leadership gurus, conferences, and trainings, because just like the classroom, physical proximity might be the single biggest factor in influencing behavior and increasing productivity in your organization. Effective leaders are engaged. They communicate. They encourage, and enthuse. They create conditions where people want to succeed. They set high standards for themselves and meet them. People around them see this and are inspired to do the same. They say people's names, smile, ask them questions about their activities, their studies, and their lives. Great leaders have to be engaged and contacting their people continuously. Leadership is a contact sport.

Leaders Work Ahead

Effective leaders stay ahead of things. Manager of two different World Series winning professional baseball teams, Tony La Russa, did this by "slowing things down to stay ahead of them" (Bissinger, 2006). While it may not seem like it sometimes, things happen fast in a professional baseball game. In a typical game, each team gets 27 outs over nine innings or three outs per inning. To slow things down, La Russa would begin his planning at the 27th out of the home team (the last out of the game) and plan his way all the way backwards to the point where his team boarded the bus to go to the ballpark. If things changed during the game, or did not go according to his plan, La Russa would repeat the process from the last out to where the change occurred. He was meticulous and considered every contingency so when something happened, he was ready for it. His method works so well Tony La Russa managed his teams to nearly 3000 wins and 2 World Series championships over his 33 years in managing.

Like La Russa (without all the wins), I always felt most effective when I stayed ahead of things. Whether it was because of my background in the military, my somewhat traditional belief that the leaders are the first ones in and the last to go home, or perhaps my own insecurity because my experience in teaching was short and I felt I needed to learn faster than my peers to catch up, I have always been in the habit of being one of the first people at work each day. To me, staying ahead starts with getting a jump on things early.

Because of this, I usually get to work about an hour early or so, check my mail-box, review my calendar for the day, return any e-mails or other correspondence, sign whatever my professional assistant had left for me to sign, and then craft a sort of thumbnail plan for who I wanted to see that day. Getting started early gives leaders the confidence that they are ready for whatever happens off script. You can be proactive even when you do not know exactly what to expect. Getting a jump on things also promotes high performance which lets both your subordinates and your peers know you have a strong grasp of your job. You are dependable and trustworthy. You do what you say and say what you mean.

About two to three times a month I will come in just a bit earlier and meet with my supervisor for buildings and grounds and walk through the school. I did this for several reasons. First, I had a wise leader tell me when you are assigned the job of principal, you are in charge of everything-not just instruction, not just teachers, not just students. Every brick, every blade of grass, and every drop of paint in the art wing are your responsibility and an effective leaders take that very seriously.

Next, I wanted the building service staff to know I cared about what they did and know their jobs were important to the functioning of our team. I was not going around looking for problems or substandard work; on the contrary! I was looking for areas I could point out for excellence and commend them for the great job they did in keeping our buildings ready for learning. Often, we would see the staff early birds which provided an additional benefit of them seeing me showing a direct and vested interest in the quality of our facility which was a plus.

Finally, the time I spent walking with my facilities supervisor allowed me to have the opportunity to forge a relationship with him and bond a bit. There is nothing like walking around at 5:30 in the morning through the immaculate, shiny halls of a beautiful school. We would speak about our families, our weekends, or vacations. We would discuss functional areas in the building and ideas for future improvements. We would also establish an open dialogue which signaled to both of us we were available for each other any time, any day and this kind of relationship between these two leaders is a must for successful school operations.

My pre-morning routine usually took about an hour and I tried to time it so I would be available about :15 minutes before the students got off the bus. I then positioned myself strategically where the most people would be entering the building so I could get the maximum amount of face-time with the arriving staff and students. For arrival, I always tried to arm myself with information about events from the previous evening (sports, concerts, awards ceremonies) so I could offer congratulations, birthdays or other milestones, and tried to be aware if anyone was struggling with anything they might need encouragement for.

Like the classroom teacher who needs to greet his or her students at the door, the school leader needs to greet the students and staff at the beginning of the day to set the tone and be on the look out for any "red flags" which could affect the day. I was always looking for students who may be acting out of character so we could get the appropriate staff member to intervene and check if they were OK. I could make some positive adjustments for things like dress code or language before they became discipline issues, and greet as many students by name as possible. This lets them know I see them and care about them and they are in a safe place where they can be themselves.

Let me digress for a minute and talk about the importance of knowing people's names. I have read and heard a number of reasons why people do not remember the names of others and they all might be valid. I am not really sure why some people are great with names while others not. I tend to be pretty decent with names, but as a building leader, there are so many stakeholders, it is difficult to know everyone to say the least. Nevertheless, the best leaders know their people well and it starts with knowing their names.

There have also been many thoughts or suggestions how to get better at remembering peoples' names. Saying it over and over when meeting someone is a good suggestion. As is associating the persons name with something you will not forget like their company or organization. Another suggestion (albeit somewhat silly) is to create an on the spot nick-name for the person you will not forget. These are all good suggestions and there are others.

The point of this digression is I cannot underestimate the power of knowing people's names. Knowing someone's name tells them you care about them and they matter to you. Just chalking up not knowing people's names to "I am just terrible with names" is weak sauce. If you are weak at it- get better because knowing people's names as a leader matters. I will also suggest you learn either first names or titles and last names ("Mr. Smith" or Ms. Jones). My friend Rob I mentioned earlier never addressed any fellow educator by anything but their title and surname. I was always impressed by it and tried to do it myself. Using just last names is disrespectful and I enthusiastically discourage the practice.

Now, in most schools the students head to class in the morning, the first bell rings, students say the pledge of allegiance, and usually there is a short string of morning announcements. Some principals I know like to be the ones who make the announcements, some schools have it done by a secretary or other staff member. One school I worked at, like many others, presented a "morning show" which was broadcasted by our Journalism Class over multi-media. Routines vary, but every school has one.

My routine in the morning was not to return immediately to my office but to spend most of the first period of the day in and out of bathrooms, classrooms, and halls. I wanted to walk a lot, smile a lot, and be on the look out for any spills, chills, and breaks so I could report them to the appropriate staff member. The school leader needs to use every opportunity for visibility. To the staff visibility means support. To the students, visibility lets them know you care and you are approachable, trusting, and kind. Finally, to the staff and students who need a bit of extra, direct supervision (we all have them), they think twice about their behavior because they know I am always out and about.

Being a contact sport means that throughout the school day, effective leaders have to take advantage of every opportunity to interact directly with staff and students. Administrators should be out in the halls at a minimum during every class change, lunch, and both at arrival as previously mentioned and dismissal. My dismissal routine was essentially my arrival routine in reverse. There is just no substitute for physical presence and the best school leaders are present.

Keep your Feedback Constructive

Class pop ins and walk throughs are also a must-do. I would set my goal at getting into as many different classrooms per day as possible and giving feedback when necessary. Let me stop here for a minute and just talk about feedback. The feedback must be constructive to be effective. Constructive means building up, not tearing down. Heck, it is in the very word *Construct*-ive. Whether you are doing walk throughs or just roaming the halls making small talk with staff, use these opportunities to build people and the organization up.

I have always been and am still opposed to using feedback to be critical unless absolutely necessary. When your feedback needs to be corrective, it needs to be meticulously planned and tactfully delivered. It also needs to include explicit instructions for improvement. In my opinion, the most important benefit of the walkthrough is to promote discourse between the walker (observer) and the teacher. When I am doing walkthroughs I am both trying to learn what is being presented and look for good teaching strategies which I can use to compliment the teacher later and share with other teachers. Usually, I'll put a quick hand-written note in the teacher's mailbox telling them how much I appreciate his or her work and use the data I collected as a way to strike up a conversation with the teacher at a later time. This usually promotes great conversations about teaching and learning and helps promote the kind of collegial relationships we desire all over the building.

This is not to say there is no value in more formal walk throughs where both qualitative and quantitative data are collected and shared in a formal setting. This kind of experience is critical for many teachers, especially the new teachers and those who are having difficulty meeting high standards and expectations. While the majority of our staff are worthy professionals, every staff has some people who

need more formal supervision, direct feedback, and

remediation than most. The worst thing we can do though is

to treat every teacher like they fall into that category when

truly there are only a few on every staff.

Of course, being present also includes attending

school events and activities. At least one member of the

school leadership team should be represented at all official

school functions after school and on weekends. Hopefully,

this goes without saying, but in the case of bigger events

(home football games, Back to School Nights, Graduation,

etc.), all members of the leadership team should be present,

professionally dressed, and having proactive, positive

interactions with the community members. School leaders

need to take every opportunity we get to show off we are

proud of our school, our students, and the job we do leading

our community. Schoolwide events provide us the perfect

opportunity. On an aside note to principals, it goes a long way to personally invite important community members to your events. Just remember to respect your chain of command. If you are going to invite board members or other high ranking public officials to your event, you want to be sure to inform the Superintendent.

Another thing a leader can do to get started towards being great is to avoid deficit leadership. I am not sure if "deficit leadership" is even a thing because I Googled it and nothing came up, so let me tell you what I think it is. Deficit leadership is looking for every deficit and trying to fix it. If we use the classroom walkthrough for an example, deficit leadership is when we do a walkthrough and then tell the teacher everything they did not do. We completely ignore their brilliant smiles, their great demeanor, their patience, their perfect format, and their salient discussion to remind them "they could have had a stronger closing activity" or "their questioning could have been more complex". This is not only a complete buzz kill, it definitely does not help anyone become a better teacher.

I remember one year I was getting evaluated as a school leader. As the person being evaluated, I was to create a portfolio of anything I thought relevant to the job I had done throughout the year to support the ratings I was to receive (I'll stop right there to just say, this is in itself is a questionable way to evaluate someone. If an evaluator cannot give me a fair, accurate evaluation based his or her own collection of data, that seems like the evaluator's deficiency). Nevertheless, I had spent a few hours putting together artifacts and examples of things I had created, initiatives I had started, and school improvement data which showed gains in nearly every statistical area. By all rights, I had an outstanding record of inputs and outcomes.

Despite all I had prepared and presented to the evaluator, the only matters which were discussed were the things I did not show evidence for to account for items in the voluminous checklist created to evaluate administrators in my state. After hours of preparation for my review, just a small amount of the conversation was spent on my presentation and the remaining time on the very few items for which I had failed to show evidence. This evaluation did little to move me forward nor did it give me any real feedback other than to tell me I better collect an artifact for every item on the checklist next year. Checklists do not grow leaders though and neither did that evaluation. This is what I see as deficit leadership.

We do this with students as well. Think about how much time we spend focusing on the "red zone" kids. You know, the ones at the very tip of the pyramid who need the most intervention. Why is it we spend so much time trying to "fix" these few kids and so little time looking specifically at what we are teaching and how it aligns to the actual assessments we are going to use to measure growth? Similarly, we spend hours observing teachers and write volumes about their teaching methods without any references to the content and whether or not it is going to even prepare the students to pass their high stakes assessments. We tend to focus very much on teacher behaviors while ignoring student behaviors and outcomes as they relate to the teacher's evaluation. These too are examples of deficit leadership and deficit leadership is bad.

They don't have to Like me, they just Need to Respect me

This phrase has been uttered by many leaders and "want to be" leaders with whom I have served in my life and nothing can be further from the truth. I do not believe you can be a most effective leader if the people you are leading do not like you. This does not mean you are "friends" with everyone, or even more than familiar. It is without a doubt

though, people will be far more willing to follow another

person for whom they have some degree of affection or

preference than someone they do not like. They might

follow a leader who is not liked because they "have" to, but it

is far better when they follow leaders because they "want"

to.

I worked with a teacher at one point in my career

with whom it was extremely difficult to warm up. For the

purpose of this story, I'll call him Mr. V. Mr. V was a very

knowledgeable teacher and athletic coach. He even enjoyed

modest success with many students and athletes. The

problem I had with him as a teacher was he struggled to get

along with his colleagues, and he found working with other

than "all- star" type students very difficult. He typically

wrote more discipline referrals than any other teacher on the

staff, and numerous students had to be removed from his

classes because he could just not get along with those who did not follow his beliefs and ideas to the letter.

Mr. V had a very negative disposition. He acted as if the world was going to end any minute and everyone was out to get him. Everything was unfair and he never got the recognition he deserved. He had a peculiar way of spelling his name and if he saw it spelled wrong, it was evidence that nobody respected him. If you have ever seen the classic *Winnie the Pooh* character Eeyore, the downtrodden donkey, this was Mr. V personified.

The first two years I spent leading Mr. V I invested a lot of time trying to give him the traditional support teachers look for. I insisted his discipline referrals were taken seriously and repeatedly took his side when there were the "he said, she said" types of incidents which happen from time to time in classrooms (seemingly more often in his). I tried coaching him, mentoring him, recognizing him for the good work he did as a teacher and a coach. Yet I could never wipe the frown from his face. I took personal time to meet with him, did walkthroughs with him, and wrote him personal notes of gratitude and encouragement.

Now, I did these kind of things with all of my teachers because they are good practices, but with Mr. V I tried extra hard to connect with him and convince him he was a valued member of the team. I encouraged him to believe he was not reaching his full potential by being so negative. Nevertheless, Mr. V still believed I did not like him and I was out to get him. He would lament on social media how difficult his job was and how nobody in leadership understood him or gave him a chance.

Ultimately, I sat down with Mr. V and had a very frank discussion. "Mr. V" I said, "We have had a lot of discussions about teaching and learning, but this one is going to be a one way conversation". I continued, "Now we are done talking and you are going to turn that frown upside down, go out there and do your job as I have directed you to do it". I concluded the conversation by telling him I did not fully know why or understand how he surmised he had things so bad, but I had done all that I could to help him overcome those feelings. I suggested he seek support from our Employee Assistance Program if he was depressed or had things going on in his personal life causing him to be so negative. I finally reminded him that when he was at work, whatever was bothering him or causing him to be so negative was unacceptable and effecting his job performance. Needless to say, while I was never Mr. V's favorite person before, he definitely did not like me after.

I tell this story to make the point that not everyone is going to like the people who lead them, sometimes no matter how benevolent or caring the leader is. In the case of Mr. V, I used everything in my bag of leadership tools to try and forge a relationship with this person, but he was just not

having it. He did not like me, and no matter how many times

I asked him how his family was, tried to create small talk

about his weekend, showed up at his athletic contests, or

encouraged him professionally, this was not going to change.

It was OK though. I gave him plenty of chances and did not

let his behavior effect mine. I ultimately did have to be open

with him regardless if it hurt his feelings.

Let me make one last point about "leaders being

liked". I contend that if you possess the leadership traits I

discussed in chapter three and you lead by the principles in

chapter four, people cannot help but respect you. If you use

the communication strategies in chapter five, and set a

personal example for health and wellness like I outlined in

chapter six, people will trust and look up to you for your

openness and discipline. Finally, if you have faith like I spoke

of in chapter seven and set your sights on continuous

personal improvement from chapter eight, people will want to follow you whether they "have to" or not. It is true, leaders do not have to be liked, but the best leaders are more than liked. They are loved and revered. People choose to follow them, are loyal to these leaders and the organization. They will do virtually anything the leader asks or suggests. They will seek opportunities for growth and seek to grow the organization. They will take initiative and do things just because it is the right thing to do. Being liked as a leader is not required, but comes naturally for the best leaders.

Chapters 10 and 11

Chapter 10 of this book will summarize the preceding chapters. You can get the "Reader's Digest" version of the entire book in chapter 10. This will be useful if you want a refresher or want someone to get a taste for the rest of the book without reading the entire book. Chapter 11 of this book will provide you with some resources which I believe

are helpful. The tool "Do More, Do Less" is designed to give

you a "go-to" of things you should do more of and less of to

be a great leader. You can even try adding your own ideas.

The tickler example I provided is very simple, but is a great

way to get started staying ahead of things especially if you

are new. I have also included a list of what I believe are

some "must reads" for aspiring readers.

I have also included a leadership self-assessment.

Feel free to recreate it and use it with your staff. Please

remember, the purpose of the tool is not for evaluation. The

purpose is for a leader to make an honest evaluation of his or

her own practices and narrow down areas for improvement.

Finally, in chapter 11 I also have had some fun with

military acronyms. The military has so many things to

remember and so many people to teach things, they use a lot

of acronyms and mnemonics to help their people remember

everything. I have listed some of these and to what they might equate in the education setting. I have relied on many of these planning and learning tools over my civilian career and I promise they will make a lot of sense. You might even use some of them yourself.

Summing it up

While I do not want to sound like an alarmist, recent times have been both complex and unpredictable for everyone across our country and the world. For many, the times have been scary and for others even worse. Times like these require the combination of human intellect, initiative, and effort which when exacerbated by great leadership can bring us to successful resolutions. The optimist in me even believes we can come out of these challenging times better than before, but it will take many of us to step up and lead.

Aggravating these conditions is the reality that the pressure on educators to be key players in helping resolve these challenges has never been higher. Moreover, I firmly believe nothing effects the quality of our lives more than an unwavering trust in God and our education. This is enormous weight on every person in our industry and is going to require not only the input of every individual, but the need for strong leaders to be able to combine the abilities of groups of people to compound the effects of their efforts.

Great leaders do many things, but what they all have in common is they accomplish their missions and they look out for the welfare of their people. Make no mistake about it, leaders who are truly leading are getting things done. This is the primary thing which makes leaders stand out. They take care of the welfare of their people because without the people in the organization, nothing can get done. So, to start improving skills as a leader, the first thing a leader can do is clarify the mission of their organization and bring the right resources to bear on that mission. The best leaders communicate the mission to every person on the team and

insist that accomplishing the mission is the only measure of

success. They establish the standard and nothing less will

suffice.

Leaders are constantly improving personally and

working on improving the skills of their team. The leadership

principles of both the Marine Corps and *Leading Made

Simple* suggest seeking self-improvement is one of the core

principles of good leadership. The best leaders see

opportunities for growth in every situation and take

advantage of every chance opportunity. This includes both

formal and informal ways of learning and honing their craft.

This also includes becoming expert in your field and in the

science and art of leadership. I was reading a book recently

about Roman Gladiators who were preparing for battle with

their foes who were just a short distance from them and

preparing in kind. The book read that "the sound of

gladiators sharpening the blades of their swords on rocks was deafening". The best leaders are constantly sharpening their swords through study, observation, reflection, and implementation.

The best leaders develop foolproof systems of organization and communication. Leaders must be depended upon to say what they mean and do what they say. This requires following up, meeting deadlines, and attending events you say you will attend. Again, one of the core leadership traits is dependability, and no leader wants to have the reputation of being undependable. The simplest way to do this is to use Tony LaRussa's theory of "slowing things down by working ahead". Think forward and work your way back from your desired outcome. Remember, Marines are master back planners and backwards planning is effective.

Finally, remember that leaders do not have to be liked, but they are usually more effective when they are. Not to worry though, if leaders adopt the traits and principles outlines here in previous chapters and throughout this book, why won't they be liked? Think for just a minute about some of the leaders you have seen who you considered the best. Did you like them or hate them (I guess there is a middle ground here)? Chances are, when you think of the best leaders with whom you have served, you at least admired and looked up to them. This is probably because they possessed an abundance of things like justice, dependability, enthusiasm, and humility. They communicated well and cared for you and your organization did great things. You probably had immense pride in your team and your school and looked upon those times as satisfying and enjoyable at the least. Great leaders don't have to be liked but the best leaders are usually loved.

Putting this into Practice

Reflection Question(s): How do the *Leading Made Simple* ideas and philosophies differ from what I have learned and/or am doing?

Suggestions for Action: Self-assess yourself using the checklist in Chapter 11. Set some specific goals to increase the frequency of the items in which you rated yourself low.

CHAPTER 10

Leading Made Simple Quick reference

Thank you for reading *Leading Educators Made Simple*. What follows is a ready reference of each of the preceding nine chapters. This is designed to help jog your memory if you need to refer to something in the book and cannot remember quite where you saw it. It can also serve as a compressed version to give you a boost when things are tough. As leaders we have a lot on our plates and a lot on our shoulders. Sometimes we need to be reminded how great it is to lead and how we can always go back to the basics to be effective. Remember as complex and difficult leading people is we can make it simple.

As we have discussed, our nation and our world may have never had a greater need for people to lead than today. The good news is while there are probably a few "born leaders" most people develop their ability to lead others through experience and training. The proof of this is that there are leaders everywhere we look. Teachers, police officers, and even moms and dads are just a few people called on to lead every day. Although there has been reams of research on leadership and what leaders do, good leadership is still somewhat of a mystery, although most of us can see whether leadership is especially bad or good.

This book provided both a pragmatic and philosophical perspective on leadership for good reason. Those interested in immediate ideas they can put right to work and those who just find leadership an interesting topic can both find something useful in the preceding pages. No matter your reason for reading though, you should be commended for your interest and commitment to using your skill as a leader to help lead teams of people to make this complex and often perplexing world a better place.

The Foundation of Every Good Leader

Every person can be a leader and improve their leadership abilities. As we have learned, most leaders are not born, they develop through training and personal experience. The two true indicators and foundation for all leadership practices are mission accomplishment and troop welfare. Mission accomplishment means meeting the expected outcome and will always outweigh troop welfare in terms of importance. We find the mission cannot usually be accomplished without the people being taken care of effectively, and this often creates a conundrum for leaders who have to balance their resources to take care of their people while reminding everyone the mission has to come first. The mission can be compared to an organizations "why". Getting everyone in the organization to commit to the same "why" is exponentially more powerful than everyone pursuing their own "why".

Traits and Principles

The best leaders seem to possess a select group of traits which make them effective. Most leaders possess these traits in varying degrees and in different combinations. The Marines have a list of what they believe are the 14 most important traits for effective leaders. The 14 traits are justice, judgement, decisiveness, integrity, dependability, tact, initiative, endurance, bearing, unselfishness, courage, knowledge, loyalty, and enthusiasm. Marines see integrity as the most important of all their leadership traits. This term, also related to dependability, means leaders do what they say and say what they mean. They never tell partial truths or white lies. One of the worst things a leader can do is not be completely honest. Trust is easily lost and difficult if not impossible to regain. While all of the leadership traits listed above are evident in the best leaders, the following five traits represent (in order) the *Leading Made Simple* traits:

Integrity, knowledge, judgement, dependability, and humility. I believe these five traits are good to emphasize (especially for new leaders) and can serve as a foundation for all good leadership practices while developing leadership and skills further.

Like the leadership traits, all good leaders follow time-tested leadership principles. Leaders learn these principles either through training, experience, and sometimes intuition. Like the traits, the Marine Corps lists eleven leadership principles. Also like the traits there are five *Leading Made Simple* leadership principles. The *Leading Made Simple* leadership principles are: 1) Set the example and model the behaviors and practices you wish to see, 2) Always reflect on your own practices and seek ways to continuously improve, 3) Know your job and do it well, 4) See everything and only do what is necessary to create the kinds of behaviors and practices you want to see, and 5) Practice

listening twice as much as speaking.

Communication

There is just no substitute for effective

communication and promoting, establishing, and maintaining

good relationships depends on a leader's ability to

communicate effectively. In fact, there may not be a more

important factor towards this effort. For *Leading Made*

Simple, I addressed communication in terms of group (mass),

interpersonal communications (individual), and briefly

touched on communicating through social media. For group

or mass communication I included sending information to

large groups of people like students, staff, parents and

communities as a whole. The keys to mass communications

vary depending on the group but one thing to be careful of is

oversaturation. Many people have a limit to how much

information they are willing to absorb. Leaders need to be

sure they are being efficient and economical in terms of how much they are asking people to listen or read.

There are four elements of interpersonal communication: listening, speaking, writing, and non-verbal. Building relationships and our effectiveness as leaders depends on each of these forms of interpersonal communication. To become a better communicator, it is important to first be self-aware. We can also enhance our communication through rehearsal, having someone proofread our written communications, video recording ourselves, or using a coach, mentor, or peer to give us feedback.

No strong communication strategy today can be complete without including social media. Many people use social media as their primary means of getting information. This is especially true with our older students. Moreover, people who use social media are connected virtually all the time and are very likely to miss any messages you send otherwise. A leader does not need to become a digital expert overnight, but must be able to implement social media as a part of their strategic communication plan for the plan to be most effective.

Health and Wellness Matters

School leadership is hard. Effective leaders must be physically and mentally fit to withstand the rigorous demands of leadership. This starts with eating healthier and being active. While no leader needs to be ready to go out and compete in the *"Iron Man World Championships"*, every leader needs to maintain his or her health through a balanced diet and normal exercise. Health and fitness not only causes us to feel better about ourselves, we actually look better, gain confidence, and can earn respect from our peers who recognize our commitment and personal discipline. Being healthy and fit can even create more time by

allowing us to make better use of the time we spend
working. When we are in better condition we are more
efficient, more effective, and can actually get more done
with the time we have.

To help make physical fitness and health a lifestyle,
go slow and make small changes. These are more likely to
stick and become permanent. There are four things you can
do to start becoming healthier right now. First reduce your
sugar intake. Next, reduce meal portion sizes. Then, increase
your level of physical activity moderately, and finally, take it
slow and make becoming healthier a long term lifestyle
change.

Another important health factor is our mental health.
Starting with the principles and practices in this book is one
way to reduce anxiety and stress. The ideas herein can help
amplify your skills as a leader increasing your productivity
and enhancing your work relationships. Then you can seek

balance in your life by spending time with family, friends, and engaging in enjoyable activities or hobbies. Finally, if increasing your efficacy at work and at home do not help, I encourage you strongly to take advantage of outside resources. Many people need the support of a counselor, therapist, or group to help them find peace, comfort, and security. Life is too short not to enjoy every minute so please seek support if you need it.

Great Leaders have Faith

Faith is what we have when we believe in someone or something we do not necessarily see. Having faith does not necessarily add to a leader's chances for success on any one endeavor, but having faith definitely affects our outlook and demeanor. Personally, I am a spiritual person. I believe in God. I pray often for His wisdom and believe to my core if God's will be done on earth, everything will be OK. For me, I put my faith in God above all other things.

If a leader does not believe in God or a higher power he or she can still have faith. Faith for this leader might be faith in expertise, training, or preparation, or faith in the great systems the leader has built. Faith may lie in believing friends or family will be there no matter what. For other leaders, faith might be in the tools or resources used to do their jobs. No matter in what a leader chooses to put his or her faith, leaders must have faith in something to motivate, inspire, and influence others.

Author Jon Gordon writes that we can choose to live our lives with faith or with fear (Gordon, 2018). Living in fear often means we almost expect the worst to happen to us (like my friend Mr. V). When we live with faith, however, we trust in something to carry us through and everything is going to be OK. Our attitude has a huge impact on our life and having faith can keep our attitude positive and pointed towards success rather than failure.

Perhaps the biggest reason we need to have faith is we have literally no idea what tomorrow brings. This seems especially during these troubling times. If we live our lives fearing that the worst is going to happen, it might! Alternatively, if we live our lives knowing we are prepared to defeat any challenge which presents itself, we know things will work out and we will succeed. Having faith simply means having confidence. We are prepared. We have the necessary resources. In my case, I am prepared by my faith in my Lord and Savior. For others they are prepared by their skills, training, and preparation. The best leaders have faith.

Constant State of Improvement

The Marine Corp Leadership principles and the *Leading Made Simple* leadership principles emphasize that the best leaders must continuously work to improve their abilities and skills. The work towards improving the leader's craft never stops. This is a foundational practice for us all.

There are many ways leaders can improve in all areas of their personal and professional lives. In addition to the many formal opportunities to learn and lead, leaders also need to take advantage of the virtually limitless informal opportunities for growth. Formal training opportunities include things like taking classes and attending seminars or conferences, entering into a formal mentoring or coaching relationship, and maybe even asking for specific feedback from your supervisor outside of official evaluations.

Informal learning opportunities are plentiful. First, leaders should use every experience as an opportunity to learn and grow. Next, leaders should seek out and maintain the company of people who can positively influence their skills and provide them resources for growth. The best leaders are always looking to move up in responsibility so they watch senior leaders and supervisors. Then, when the time comes to step in and do the jobs of their supervisor, the leader is ready.

Leaders are readers. Leaders read for the technical knowledge, to remain up to date in the industry, and for entertainment. Not only do leaders learn from reading, reading improves our written and verbal communication skills like diction and vocabulary. Reading exercises our mind just like activity exercises our muscles. Reading can help reduce stress, increase concentration, and improve memory too. Leaders are readers.

Few things expand and reinforce something we know like teaching it to another person. To that end, leaders seize opportunities to share and teach with their colleagues. Leaders in education can never forget they are teachers and teacher leaders so they hone their craft by taking advantage of opportunities to prepare and present lessons. Leaders should also seek a coach and be a coach. Skilled coaches objectively let us know how we can improve or help us arrive

at this information through a series of deliberate questions.

Serving as a coach for someone else keeps our skills sharp

and increases our opportunities for dialogue with other

leaders.

Take it Next Level

There is no need to exaggerate the challenges,

complexity, and unpredictability of our recent past. For some

people these times have been frightening and for many

others even tragic. At the least we have all lost something

even if nothing more than time with loved ones or

opportunities to participate in activities we enjoy. We have

overcome previous challenges in our history by combining

human intellect, initiative, and effort along with great

leadership. When human beings have joined together for a

common purpose we have shown the resolve and ability to

overcome all previous challenges and tragedies. We have

suffered through world wars, other pandemics, economic

depressions, and civil war. In the end we have always come

through. The optimist in me even believes we can come out

of these challenging times too, but we will need to step up

and lead.

Aggravating these modern conditions for us in

education is the reality that the pressure on educators to be

key players in helping resolve these challenges has never

been higher. Our society, which already demanded so much

from our educators has not lessened it's demands.

Compounding this is the fact we have been forced to learn

how to teach in a completely different environment, while

continuing to teach. We do this is because we know nothing

on earth effects the quality of our students' lives and the

quality of our entire society more than education. This puts

pressure on every person in every school and amplifies the

need for strong leaders to be able to combine the abilities of all groups of people to compound the effects of their individual efforts.

Great leaders are judged by many factors, but the truest indicators of effective leadership are mission accomplishment and taking care of people. Did the leader get the job done? This is the primary qualifier for making leaders stand out. They also know they need to take care of the welfare of their people because without the people, nothing can get accomplished. To start improving skills as a leader, the first thing a leader should do is clarify the mission of their organization and then collect and collaborate the use of all resources in a common effort. Leaders should communicate the mission to every person on the team and demand that accomplishing the mission is the primary and uncompromised measure of success.

Leaders are constantly seeking self-improvement and improving their team. The leadership principles of both the

Marine Corps and *Leading Made Simple* suggest seeking self-improvement as one of the core principles of good leadership. The best leaders find opportunities for growth in all circumstances and use every opportunity as a chance to grow. Growth includes both formal and informal opportunities to enhance and sharpen skills. Leaders should become both an expert in their field and in the science and art of leadership. This can only be accomplished through explicit, daily effort towards self-improvement.

The best leaders develop infallible structures of organization and communication. Leaders are reliable and say what they mean and do what they say. They are counted on to follow, meet deadlines, and attend events they say they will attend. Again, one of the core leadership traits is dependability, and no leader wants to have the reputation of not being dependable. The simplest way to start becoming more organized (and save yourself a lot of angst) is to use

Tony LaRussa's theory of "slowing things down by working ahead". Constantly thinking forward and working back from the end helps slow things down so everything does not seem to be happening at once. Marines are master back planners and backwards planning is effective.

Finally, remember that leaders do not have to be liked, but the most effective leaders usually are. The good news is, if leaders apply the traits and principles outlines in the preceding chapters why wouldn't he or she be liked? Think for just a minute about some of the best leaders with whom you have worked. Did you like them or dislike them? I am guessing the former, because usually when you think of the best leaders with whom you have served, you looked up to them and enjoyed giving them your very best.

This is very likely because they possessed an abundance of the effective leadership traits like justice, dependability, enthusiasm, and humility. Their messages

were clear and they demonstrated care for your welfare.
They cared for the organization too and did great things. I
would guess as you reflect on your favorite experiences with
a leader, you probably had pride in your team, pride in your
school, and looked upon those times as satisfying and
enjoyable. Great leaders don't have to be liked but the best
leaders are usually loved.

Putting this into Practice

Reflection Question(s): How would you phrase the "big idea"
after reading the preceding chapters? Can you think of and
phrase any other big ideas from this book?

Suggestions for Action: List three tangible practices from
what you have read you can adopt and implement today.

CHAPTER 11

Tools and Resources

Do More Do Less List- To avoid deficit leadership I have changed the traditional "Do's and Don'ts" list to a "Do More, Do Less" list. To improve your leadership do more of the things on the left.

Do More	Do Less
Get out and make physical contact with people	Spend time at your desk
Smile	Criticize
Listen	Talk
Tell the truth always	Bend the truth or tell white lies
Work ahead	Avoid things you do not like
Learn about your people	Micromanage
Learn about your craft	Look for things that are wrong
Ask questions	Say No
Stay active- Exercise	Complain
Improve your health and diet	Show favoritism
Congratulate- Praise	Nit-pick
Collaborate	Go at things alone

Own it!	Blame things out of your control
Share your knowledge and resources	Be guarded or protectionist
Stay organized	Shoot from the hip
Grow personally and professionally	Remain stagnate
Have faith	Have or use fear
Have time for people	Be impatient
Teach/share your knowledge	Avoid additional leadership opportunities
Love and spend time with your family	Put too much value on your work

Recommended Readings

Culturize. (2017). By Casas, J.

Drive. (2009). By Pink, D.

Holy Bible. New International Version.

Leaders Eat Last. (2017). By Sinek, S.

Leverage Leadership. A Practical Guide to Building Exceptional Schools. (2012). By Bambrick-Santoyo, P. and Peider, B.

Multipliers. How the Best leaders Make Everyone Smarter.

(2010). By Mckeown, G. and Wiseman, L.

Relationships 101. What Every Leader Needs to Know. (2003).

By Maxwell, J.C.

School Culture Rewired. How to Define, Assess, and

Transform it. (2015). By Gruenert, S. & Whitaker, T.

Start with Why. (2011). By Sinek, S.

The Case for Christ. A Journalist's Personal Investigation of

the Evidence for Jesus. (1998). By Strobel, L.

The Energy Bus. 10 Rules to Fuel your Life, Work, and Team with Positive Energy. (2007). By Gordon, J.

The Power of a Positive Team. (2018). By Gordon, J.

What Great Teachers Do Differently. 17 Things that Matter Most. (2nd. Ed.). (2013). By Whitaker, T.

What Great Principals Do Differently. 18 Things that Matter Most. (2nd ed.) (2013). By Whitaker, T.

This is a short list of leadership books I have read and recommend. I am sure there are many other great books and inspirational authors, but I chose to only include books which I have personally read. I listed them alphabetically by title so they are easy to search.

Sample Tickler

Having a foolproof method of staying organized is a must for any leader. As you move up, you might have the benefit of an assistant or office professional to help. Many people today live through electronic medium. Frankly, the platforms for electronic organization are preferred. If you are one who need a list in front of you, here is an idea to keep your tasks organized and your priorities. Check out the example of a "tickler" I liked to use beforel I became adept with technology.

Example

Steven Lucas   **Date**

Yearly Goals:

1) **Increase percentage of underrepresented students in advanced placement courses.**

2) **Increase the percentage of passing grades in 10th grade.**

3) **Decrease the number of out of school suspension days for students in 10th grade.**

Tickler

Task	DUE DATE
Put tasks and to-dos here. Add rows if needed.	Include dates!

Quote: The greatest good you can do for another is not just to share your riches, but reveal to them their own. -Benjamin Disraeli

Marine Corps Leadership Traits and Principles

Traits (14)

Justice	Judgement	Decisiveness	Dependability	Integrity
Tact	Initiative	Endurance	Bearing	Unselfishness
Courage	Knowledge	Loyalty	Enthusiasm	

Principles (11)

1) Know yourself and seek self-improvement.

2) Be technically and tactically proficient.

3) Know your Marines and look out for their welfare.

4) Keep your Marines informed.

5) Set the Example.

6) Ensure the task is understood, supervised, and accomplished.

7) Train your Marines as a team.

8) Make sound and timely decisions.

9) Develop a sense of responsibility among your subordinates.

10) Employ your command in accordance with its

capabilities.

11) Seek responsibility and take responsibility for your

actions.

Leading Made Simple Traits and Principles

To make things a bit easier, I have narrowed down the list of traits and principles to the five most impactful and to which I refer to as the *Leading Made Simple* traits and principles. While all of the Marine Corps traits and principles are important and can support your improvement as a leader, the *Leading Made Simple* traits and principles listed below are a great place to start.

Leading Made Simple Traits (5)

Integrity, Knowledge, Judgement, Dependability, and Humility

Leading Made Simple Principles (5)

1) Set the example and model the behaviors and practices you wish to see.

2) Always reflect on your own practices and seek ways

to continuously improve.

3) Know your job and do it well.

4) See everything and only do what is necessary to

create the kinds of behaviors and practices you want

to see.

5) Practice listening twice as much as speaking.

***Leading Made Simple* Leadership Self-Assessment**

Check the box which rank how often you exhibit the trait or

follow the principle.

ITEM	Need to do More			Do Sometimes				Do Mostly or Always		
	1	2	3	4	5	6	7	8	9	10
Act with integrity										
Have knowledge of my job										
Employ effective leadership skills										
Make accurate decisions (Judgement)										
Do what I say and say what I mean (dependability)										
Approach things from a novice										

perspective (humility)									
Set a sterling personal example									
Continuously seek self-improvement									
See everything and do only what is necessary to influence behavior									
Listen twice as much as I talk									

Fun with Acronyms and Mnemonics

Marines and their friends in the other military organizations love acronyms and mnemonics to help them remember the many procedures they follow to get things done. I have listed a few and how they are used and how they can be useful in the education setting.

ADDIE

A- Analyze

D- Design

D- Develop

I- Implement

E-Evaluate

I first learned the acronym ADDIE at a curriculum development course produced by the Navy. The acronym is still useful for me today and I use it a lot in planning events and of course when creating professional development or other training related events.

SMEAC

S- Situation (What is going on?)

M- Mission (What do we have to do?)

E- Execution (How will we do it?)

A- Administration and Logistics (What do we need to get it done?)

C- Command and Signal (How will we communicate and who is in charge?)

SMEAC is the grand-daddy acronym and every Marine knows it. This is the mission order and when used properly can account for every detail of any event regardless of its size or scope. Using this for any plan helps ensure nothing is forgotten.

4 Bs- Logistics

B- Beans

B- Bullets

B- Bandages

B- Bad Guys

The 4 Bs are used to ensure we have taken care of all of the logistical needs. The 4 Bs fits into the mission order above under Administration and Logistics. We can still use this in education by replacing a couple words.

4 Bs for education

B- Beans (Child Nutrition Services)

B- Books (Al instructional materials and technology)

B- Bandages (School nurse or other medical needs)

B- Boys and Girls (Our students of course!)

BAMCIS- Leadership Steps

B- Begin the Planning

A- Arrange the reconnaissance

M- Make the reconnaissance

C- Complete the plan

I- Issue the mission order

S- Supervise

BAMCIS are the six troop leading steps and maybe the second most well-known acronym. Like the mission order (SMEAC), BAMCIS gives the leader a sort of step by step tool so they do not forget anything. I have changed it below for education.

B- Began to plan

A- Arrange to review the planning process

M- Meet with your team

C- Complete the Plan

I- Issue instructions to everyone

S- See that everything is done to fidelity

Here are some which probably will not help you but might make you smile!

1stCivDiv- The duty station every Marine cannot wait to report to- Home!

Ant Farm- Location, usually high on a hill where antennas are deployed for communications.

BCD- Bad Conduct Discharge. Also referred to as the "Big Chicken Dinner".

DI- Drill Instructor (of course!). Drill Instructors prefer "Drill Instructor" to "DI" which Marines will sometimes use to mean "Dumb Idiot". To some Marines they are the same thing!

Doc- Anyone in the medical or dental field. Usually a Navy person.

FUBAR- Fouled Up Beyond Repair (Marines have been known to use another word in place of "Fouled")

IP- Irish pennants. The sometimes tiny strings which hang from the seems of Marine's uniforms. They detract from perfect appearance and are "hits" in any inspection.

MOPP gear- Equipment worn to protect Marines from the

effects of nuclear, biological, and chemical attack.

PFT- Physical Fitness test. Done twice a year, this is the most

fun a Marine can have in an hour.

UCMJ- The Uniform Code of Military Justice. No Marine

wants to be subject to the UCMJ!

CHAPTER 12

The Author

Steven Lucas grew up in a suburban community and was the benefactor of good public schools and good parents. Unfortunately, youth and ignorance kept the young man from taking advantage of these conditions so when he graduated from high school in the early eighties, Steve, thinking he was smarter than everyone else, took a job at a local factory with visions of making a lot of money and living the adult world free from rules and restrictions.

As we have all learned, adult life is hard, and it is harder if you are naïve, or even stupid. Steve found, without an education, training, or experience, the best he could do was work in a low paying job for nominal benefits and little satisfaction. Within a year he knew he needed to do something different, but now detached from school, and being from a traditional blue-collar family which had little understanding of the many opportunities for education and training, he did not know exactly what was next.

The Marine Corps offered Steve the opportunity for training, adventure, and the chance to challenge himself. So, in 1983 Steve shipped off for Marine Corps Recruit Training at the Marine Corps Recruit Depot in San Diego, California. 12 weeks later Steve graduated and began a career in which he grew both in spirit and in ability. The Marines gave Steve the purpose, the challenge, and the outlet for his enthusiasm for life which had been lacking before.

Following his retirement from the Marines in 2003, Steve completed his Master of Education degree at the University of Illinois and began his second career in Education. Steve's career in public education, while short compared to many of his peers, has been full. Steve has served as a classroom teacher, Assistant Principal, School Principal, and District Superintendent.

Steve is very proud of his accomplishments as a life-

long learner. He will tell you he earned his Bachelor of

Science degree literally going to school nights, on weekends,

taking assessments, and matriculating anything into credit he

could find. He did this while serving on active duty,

sometimes working a second job officiating sports or

delivering pizzas, and raising a family. After Steve's

retirement from the Marines, he earned his Master of

Education degree from the University of Illinois in much the

same manner. Steve has also earned a post graduate

certification in Educational Leadership from the College of

Notre Dame of Maryland and a Doctor of Education in

Leadership from the American College of Education.

Steve is the course Honor Graduate from the United

States Marine Corps Drill Instructor School, the Staff Non-

Commissioned Officer's Leadership Academy, and the

Advanced Staff Non-Commissioned Officer's Leadership

Academy. He is also a graduate of the Federal Bureau of

Investigation's National Academy (FBINA) and a Master

Fitness Specialist trained by the Cooper Institute in Dallas, TX.

He is an avid reader, writer, and enjoys being active with his

wife Stephanie and his daughter, Grace. Steve gives all

thanks, praise, and glory to the Lord of his life Jesus Christ.

Works Cited

Anspaugh, D. (Director). (1993). *Rudy.* Film. DVD Release.

Bissinger, B. (2006). *Three Nights in August: Strategy,*

Heartbreak, and Joy Inside the Mind of a Manager.

Houghton Mifflin Company, Boston, MA.

Casas, J. (2017). *Culturize.* Dave Burgess Consulting, Inc. San

Diego, CA.

Gordon, J. (2018). *The Power of a Positive Team.* John Wiley

and Sons Inc. Hoboken, NJ.

Guwande, A. (2017). *Want to get Great at Something? Get a*

Coach. Ted Talk retrieved from

https://www.ted.com/talks/atul_gawande_want_to_

get_great_at_something_get_a_coach?language=en

Maxwell, J.C. (2003). *Relationships 101. What Every Leader*

Needs to Know. Thomas Nelson Inc.

Nashville, TN.

MCIP 3-10A.4i. (2020). Marine Rifle Squad. Retrieved from

https://www.marines.mil/Portals/1/Publications/MC

IP%203-10A.4i%20wChg1.pdf?ver=2020-05-22-

085455-150

MCRP 6-11B. (2008). Marine Corps Values: Appendix A, B.

retrieved from

https://www.fitness.marines.mil/Portals/211/Docs/F

FI/MCRP%206-

11B%20%20W%20CH%201%20Marine%20Corps%20

Values_A%20User's%20Guide%20for%20Discussion%

20Leaders.pdf

Pink, D.H. (2009). *Drive*. Penguin Group. New York, NY.

Sayers, G. and Silverman, A. (1970, 2001). *I am Third: The

Inspiration for Brian's Song*. Penguin Books.

New York, NY.

Sinek, S. (2011). *Start with Why*. Portfolio Penguin. New York,

NY.

Sinek, S. (2017). *Leaders Eat Last.* Portfolio/Penguin. New

York, NY.

Whitaker, T. (2013). *What Great Teachers Do Differently. 17*

Things that Matter Most. (2nd. Ed.).

Routledge. New York, NY.

Whitaker, T. (2013). *What Great Principals Do Differently. 18*

Things that Matter Most. (2nd ed.).

Routledge. New York, NY.